the Sports Car book

First published in February 2007

A catalogue record for this book is available from the British Library

ISBN 978 1 84425 325 8

Library of Congress catalog card no 2006933583

Published by Haynes Publishing, Sparkford,
Yeovil, Somerset BA22 7JJ, UK

Tel: 01963 442030 Fax: 01963 440001
Int. tel: +44 1963 442030 Int. fax: +44 1963 440001
E-mail: sales@haynes.co.uk
Website: www.haynes.co.uk

Haynes North America Inc.,
861 Lawrence Drive, Newbury Park,
California 91320, USA

Printed and bound in Great Britain by
J. H. Haynes & Co. Ltd, Sparkford

WARNING
While every attempt has been made throughout this book to
emphasise the safety aspects of working on a car, the publishers,
the author and the distributors accept no liability whatsoever for any
damage, injury or loss resulting from the use of this book. If you have
any doubts about your ability to safely work on a car then it is
recommended that you seek advice from a professional engineer.

Jurisdictions which have strict emission control laws may consider
the running of certain vehicles or any modifications to a vehicle to be
an infringement of those laws. You are advised to check with the
appropriate body or authority whether your proposed purchase or
modification complies fully with the law. The publishers accept no
liability in this regard.

the Sports Car book

The essential guide to buying, owning, enjoying and maintaining a sports car

Paul Guinness

1

Sports car **scene**

2

Living with a sports car

3

Running a sports car

7

Buying a used sports car

8

Classic collection

9

Buying restoring, maintaining

Brand new **options**

Buying a new sports car

Second-hand **sector**

Add-ons & upgrades

Introduction

Today's sports car scene is one that combines fascination and enthusiasm with a glorious blurring of the edges between the different genres. That's because fans of proper sports cars tend to be just that, less bothered by whether a certain model is seen as classic or contemporary, more concerned with the sheer thrill and enjoyment to be gained from driving such a beast.

Back in 1986 I was given my first full-time job in motoring journalism, as Editorial Assistant on the now defunct *Sports Car Monthly* magazine. A happy year was spent writing sports car features and driving countless new and used examples, although back then the sports car scene was a far less healthy place to be than it is today. It was, after all, a full three years before the debut of the Mazda MX-5, the car largely responsible for the renaissance of the sports car market throughout the 1990s and beyond.

My professional introduction to sports cars had quite an effect, and the whole scene has been a major part of my life ever since. And I'm not alone. These days, there are more fans of the sports car concept than ever before, and it's easy to see what the attraction is. Take any well-sorted two-seater convertible, drive it the way it was designed to be driven, revel in the joys of open-air motoring all over again, and you'll agree that a proper sports car is still the

OPPOSITE The sports car scene has rarely looked healthier – and one of today's top used buys is the much-loved second-generation Mazda MX-5. *(Mazda)*

ABOVE Bringing the fun back to your motoring, no matter how large or small your budget, is what *The Sports Car Book* is all about. *(Porsche)*

LEFT A classic sports car can be a tempting proposition, but which ones make the most sense? You'll find plenty of advice here. *(Author)*

most effective way of bringing the fun back to motoring.

What The *Sports Car Book* sets out to do is bring to life the entire sports car scene, and it should prove particularly useful if you're considering buying your very first sports car. Do you go for a brand new model or buy second-hand? Should you consider a classic, and what are the pros and cons? What are the points to look for when buying used? How do you go about insuring your newly acquired sports car? And exactly which models are out there, best suited to your particular needs? These and many other questions are answered in *The Sports Car Book*.

Many of today's sports car fans will appreciate any well-developed, fun to drive sportster, irrespective of its 'classic', 'new', or 'second-hand' status. And in a motoring world where badge snobbery and upmarket aspirations seem to rule, this all goes to make a refreshing change.

Whether it's a basic and charming MG Midget from the 1970s, a first-generation Mazda MX-5 from the '90s, or a brand new Porsche Boxster that takes your fancy, you're in good company. The world of sports cars has never been so diverse, and rarely so healthy. It's a great time to join the clan; get out there and put the fun back into your motoring. Life can be way too serious at times.

What is a sports car?

If you've just spent your own money on this book and are about to start reading it in earnest, you're almost certainly either a sports car fan already and want to learn more about the breed, or you're

BELOW If neck-snapping performance and raw exhilaration are what you crave, the Caterham Seven still takes some beating. *(Caterham)*

thinking of taking your first plunge into sports car ownership. Either way, you're in good company. Today's various sports car scenes – new, used, and classic – are both fascinating and diverse; and for the sheer number of tempting and varied sports cars available for all budgets, there's never been a better time to buy.

The first dilemma with any book such as this, of course, is deciding which cars to include and which to leave out. I mean, what exactly is a sports car? Can an accomplished hot hatch like a VW Golf GTi be considered a sports car, for instance? Maybe, but not for the purposes of this book. Similarly, does the fact that a car is some kind of convertible automatically make it a sports car? Not in our opinion, for that would mean such models as the Peugeot 307 CC being included as sports cars – which plainly they're not.

Narrowing down the genre isn't always easy, but here we'll be concentrating solely on two-seater convertibles – and, in particular, those that can be considered true sports cars (at least, as far as we're concerned). They might not all be raw and raucous in the Caterham Seven sense, but they all deserve a place in the book for one reason or another. They might not all be high-performance machines either, but – as we'll learn further on – a sports car doesn't have to be the fastest car on the block to be considered fun and a worthwhile buy.

The other dilemma we had to face up to when planning *The Sports Car Book* was what budget cut-off point should be applied. Should a nearly new soft-top Porsche 911 be given coverage, for example, when it's financially beyond the reach of many enthusiasts? And at the other end of the scale, we had to consider whether or not to include sports cars costing no more than what you'd pay for a decent sofa – or even less.

The end result? Well, we love sports cars. We're obsessed with the things, almost irrespective of their make, model, age, and value. So this book will be all-encompassing, bringing together a wealth of information, advice, and sheer entertainment covering just about all the sports cars on your own personal shortlist – no matter how healthy or otherwise your budget might be.

Acknowledgements

Researching and writing a book that encompasses all aspects of the sports car scene is a hefty task, so I'm grateful to everybody who offered advice, help and encouragement along the way.

Among the many names I could mention, I'd particularly like to thank Rod Jones, Frank Westworth, and Jose Gonzalez Garcia for their unstinting support throughout.

I'm also indebted to Haynes Publishing's Mark Hughes, Steve Rendle, and Christine Smith for their professional help and personal encouragement throughout this and all other projects.

Finally, to all the hardworking folk in the various car company press offices who have provided information and countless road-test vehicles over the years, a heartfelt thank you.

I hope all budding sports car enthusiasts enjoy what follows …

Paul Guinness
January 2007

Sports car
scene

How do you define a sports car? For the purposes of this book, we're restricting ourselves to two-seater convertibles. *(Honda)*

Sports car **heaven**

There are some things in life you never forget your first experience of. Sex is one. And your very first drive in a proper two-seater ragtop sports car is another. It almost doesn't matter what make or model it is, as long as it's a well-sorted example of a decent design. Whether that means a freshly restored MG Midget Mk III, a low-mileage Series I Mazda MX-5, an all-wheel drive Audi TT, or a free-revving Honda S2000, the experience will leave you craving another such thrilling drive.

There's something about the low-down driving position of a proper two-seater soft-top sportster that brings out the enthusiast in everyone – even if it's a relatively low-powered Mazda MX-5 from the early 1990s. Here's a car that doesn't seem all that exciting when you look at its on-paper performance figures, particularly if it's a lowly 1.6-litre version. But once you've climbed aboard, got yourself settled into the snug but comfortable cockpit, fired up the ever-eager four-pot motor and watched how readily the rev counter flicks towards the red line, you suddenly get an inkling you're in for a more enjoyable experience than you first expected.

And that's the joy of so many of today's sports cars, particularly on the second-hand market. At the affordable end of the scene, you'll usually be able to find a hot hatch that – in terms of official figures – will be able to outperform your own choice of two-seater sports car. But that hot hatch won't have the same driver appeal, particularly on the kind of winding B-roads that are the natural habitat of the best sports cars out there.

The way a rear-wheel-drive MX-5 handles its power, for example, is exemplary. You've got strong enough acceleration for most buyers, combined with fantastically communicative handling and grippy roadholding that only a really well designed two-seater sports car can provide – aided and abetted by the breed's low centre of gravity. Push the car too hard and you'll find a back end that's not afraid to drift slightly, but is easily brought back under control with a touch of opposite lock and a blip of the accelerator. It brings out the very best driver in you, and brings real entertainment value back to your motoring.

Still not convinced? Still adamant that a Golf GTi will provide superior acceleration and a more rapid top speed than a similarly priced MX-5? You

could be right. But don't fall into the trap of reading more into on-paper performance figures than they deserve. A well-engineered hot hatch can be a rapid machine, with handling and grip to match. But what it so often lacks is communication, charisma, and a feeling that you're making even more rapid progress. With a two-seater sports car, you don't necessarily have to be driving ultra-fast to be having enormous fun behind the wheel. A proper sports car provides entertainment by the bucket load.

A German-built hot hatch might be well built, quick (if you're lucky), and very competent in all it does. But it almost certainly won't have that special 'X Factor' that only a two-seater sports car can provide. That feeling of ultimate fun. That desire to take to the road just for the sheer hell of it.

OPPOSITE A proper sports car doesn't need to be ultra fast in order to put a smile on your face, and the classic MG Midget is proof of this. *(Author)*

BELOW The original Mazda MX-5 wasn't about ultimate power or on-paper performance. It was its all-round fun factor that really counted – and still does. *(LAT)*

Development
of the sports car

The idea of a two-seater sports car isn't a new one. In fact, almost from the day the motor car was invented there have been enthusiasts who've yearned for a sportier, faster, more exciting version. And over the years manufacturers have been only too happy to oblige.

Prior to World War 2, exciting sports car designs were pouring out of factories run by the likes of Bentley, MG, Morgan, and Sunbeam, making Britain the world's most successful sports car manufacturer in the process. But it was the best of the post-war models that eventually saw the world's sports car scene start expanding at an unprecedented rate.

With no new models available for launch immediately after the war, pre-war designs were hastily upgraded and put back into production in a desperate attempt by manufacturers to revive their civilian market. But the pressure was on to create brand new, up-to-the-minute replacements for these ageing models – and not just in the UK.

Britain was, of course, desperate to remain the frontrunner in terms of sports car design and

OPPOSITE The sports car concept is almost as old as the motor car itself. Here's the original MG ('Old Number One') winning the 1925 Land's End Trial, its first motor sport success. *(MG Rover)*

LEFT MG's highly successful T-series line-up was a hit with sports car fans worldwide, both prior to World War 2 and right through until 1955. *(Author)*

BELOW The arrival of the MGA in the mid-1950s brought modernity to the famous MG marque, and proved an instant hit on both sides of the Atlantic. *(MG Rover)*

ABOVE The XK140 Roadster may not have hit the streets until 1954, but the exciting new Jaguar XK120 was making its debut as early as 1949. *(Jaguar)*

RIGHT The arrival of the MGB in '62 was an important event. Over the next 18 years, this would be one of the company's best-selling sports cars of all time. *(MG Rover)*

RIGHT Remember the Lotus Seven, predecessor of the Caterham? It dates back to 1957, this example – famous for its role in TV's cult series *The Prisoner* – is from '65. *(Caterham Cars)*

FAR RIGHT Renault's Caravelle and Floride convertibles brought some much-needed sexiness to the French car maker's line-up during the 1960s. *(Renault)*

manufacturing. But the smaller companies knew they couldn't afford to create exciting all-new designs overnight, while the larger corporations knew they had to place their emphasis on bigger-selling family saloons before they could turn their attention to the sports car market. That's why the legendary name of MG found itself with a warmed-up pre-war sports car range (in the shape of the TC, TD, and TF) right through until 1955, the year when the eagerly anticipated new MGA finally hit the streets – a full decade after the end of World War 2.

The 1950s saw some frenzied activity in the sports car market, with sales-grabbing British newcomers like the 1953 Austin-Healey 100 and Triumph TR2, the 1954 Jaguar XK140 Roadster, the 1955 Triumph TR3, the 1957 Lotus Seven, the 1958 Austin-Healey Sprite and MGA Twin Cam, and the 1959 Sunbeam Alpine all bringing fresh new excitement to the sporting scene. And during the same decade, of course, America's General Motors was busy launching the now-legendary first-generation Chevrolet Corvette, Germany's Porsche was doing rather nicely with its superb 356A Speedster, and Italy's Alfa Romeo was making a sports car name for itself with the delightful Giulietta Spider of 1955 and the 2000 Spider of '58. The sports car scene was taking off in a big way everywhere.

That, though, was nothing compared with what happened in the '60s, one of the most exciting decades ever in terms of music, fashion, culture … and sports cars. New two-seaters appeared in their droves, with Britain once again providing some big hits thanks to the Austin-Healey Sprite Mk II and its MG Midget badge-engineered cousin; the larger MGB of 1962, replacement for the MGA; the affordable new Triumph Spitfire and its more expensive relatives, the TR4, TR4A, TR5, and TR6 that appeared as the decade progressed; the V8-powered Morgan Plus 8 of 1968; the outrageous new AC Cobra with its world-beating supercar performance; the truly entertaining Lotus Elan; and, of course, the legendary Jaguar E-Type, which in convertible guise is still credited as being one of the sexiest, most beautiful cars of all time. With newcomers

like those appearing throughout the decade, this was truly the heyday of the British two-seater sports car.

But the genre wasn't just proving a hit in Britain: other countries and their manufacturers were keen to get in on the action. Alfa Romeo's brand new Duetto Spider of 1966 was one of the prettiest little convertibles money could buy;

ABOVE The gorgeous Alfa Romeo Duetto Spider proved the Italians knew a thing or two about fun-to-drive sports cars. These days it's considered an all-time classic. *(Alfa Romeo)*

ABOVE It might not have been a full convertible, but the new Porsche 911 Targa provided its own style of open-top motoring to anybody with a large enough bank balance. *(Porsche)*

Renault's Caravelle Convertible was providing Francophiles with a handsome and fairly upmarket option; Porsche's Targa version of its desirable new 911 was providing open-air motoring with all the benefits of a steel roof; Mercedes-Benz's SL series of 1963 brought Germanic opulence to those with a healthy budget; Honda wowed the world with its first ever sports cars, the diminutive but hugely fun S600 and S800 models; Fiat's delightful 124 Spider and 850 Spider provided Italian charisma aplenty; and for those with drastically more money than the masses, awe-inspiring Ferraris like the 365 California and 365 GTS combined stunning looks with outrageous-for-the-time performance.

RIGHT When the MG Midget and Austin-Healey Sprite Mk II bounced onto the scene, they brought fun, sporty motoring to those on a tight new-car budget. *(MG Rover)*

Start of the **decline**

But despite such promising progress via numerous manufacturers, the following decade would prove to be a disappointment for many enthusiasts, with the 1970s being best described as an era of stagnation for some of the world's most famous marques.

And none more so than MG, whose biggest claim to fame during the decade (apart from launching a V8-engined version of the B GT model) was to conform to new American safety legislation by raising the ride height of its Midget and B models and fitting monstrous black bumpers in place of the pretty chrome originals. Such action was a necessary evil, though, if MG was to maintain a sales presence in its most important world market: the USA.

Triumph, like MG, was part of the British Leyland empire by the time the 1970s hove into view – and for its sports car sales it, too, had relied on the American market for many years. But with safety legislation in the States becoming ever more

ABOVE Datsun showed the world how to build a decent six-cylinder sports car with the arrival of the 240Z. Just imagine how impressive a convertible version would have been ... *(Nissan)*

stringent and widespread talk of convertibles being
banned altogether in that most crucial of markets,
Triumph's eventual replacement for the hairy-
chested TR6 convertible was a wedge-shaped
four-cylinder hard-top coupé going by the name of
TR7. That was back in 1975; and by the time a
soft-top version of the TR7 did finally appear four
years later it was all too late for what had become

a hopelessly unreliable and highly criticised
product.

Launched the same year as the TR7 was the
important new Jaguar XJ-S, effectively the
replacement for the now-legendary E-Type – but a
model that initially failed to live up to its
predecessor's enviable image. Replacing the
E-Type was never going to be easy; but the fact

ABOVE Another coupé crying out to be made a full convertible many years before it actually happened was Jaguar's controversial new XJ-S. *(Jaguar)*

LEFT As the 1970s drew to a close, so did the life of the MG Midget. The final example rolled out of the Abingdon (England) factory in '79. *(British Leyland)*

that the XJ-S was available only in two-door coupé guise for the first few years of its life was almost an insult to those who yearned for another soft-top sporting Jaguar.

As a point of interest, it was the threat of the anti-convertible movement in America that was largely to blame for the demise of the Austin-Healey name by the end of the 1960s. It seemed pointless developing a successor to the rapidly ageing Austin-Healey 3000 if its main market was to be taken away from it, so the 1970s saw no new Austin-Healeys being developed – and the beginning of the end for other models, too. By the end of the decade, time had finally been called on the long-neglected but still likeable MG Midget, its final example rolling off the production line in 1979.

The rot had truly set in at Abingdon, the site of MG's famous factory.

Some manufacturers had sporting successes in the '70s, though, with Nissan's highly praised new 240Z proving a massive hit around the globe. This car proved that a Japanese designed and built sportster could take on the established giants from Britain, Italy, and America – and beat them at their own game. In fact, it didn't take long for the 240Z to become the world's best-selling sports car of its era, with many pundits describing this six-cylinder gem as the spiritual successor to the Austin-Healey 3000. For a Japanese company new to the concept of best-selling sports cars, that was praise indeed. It's just a pity that, for the purposes of *The Sports Car Book,* a ragtop version was never offered.

If the 1970s had its fair share of sports car bad times, the '80s was positively disastrous as far as many enthusiasts were concerned. In fact, the decade got off to the worst of sporting starts when the antiquated MG factory at Abingdon finally shut up shop and the very last MGB rolled out of the gates. In production for 18 years, the B had proved a major success for MG and its parent, British Leyland. But having suffered from chronic underdevelopment and lack of investment in its later years, the B's demise was a sad inevitability.

Triumph's Spitfire and TR7 models weren't far behind, with production ceasing in 1980 and 1981 respectively, bringing to an end a long and successful era of two-seater Triumph sports cars. The car market was changing rapidly, and the traditional two-seater sports car was suffering as a result.

The **hot hatch** effect

Almost certainly it was the arrival of the Volkswagen Golf GTi in the late '70s and the massive expansion of the hot hatch market throughout the 1980s that spelled the end for a number of previously popular two-seaters. The arrival of the hot hatch brought sports car performance in a four-seater, practical package – and the trendiest buyers of the 1980s couldn't get enough of the new breed.

VW Golf GTi, Ford Escort XR3i, Peugeot 205 GTi, Vauxhall Astra/Opel Kadett GSE, Renault 5 GT Turbo, Fiat Uno Turbo … they all proved major hits, each one contributing to the (thankfully fairly short-term) decline in the traditional sports car market. Two-seater convertibles were out. The hot hatch was the new king of the tarmac.

Having said that, a number of traditional sports cars did make it successfully through the 1980s, with the Alfa Romeo Spider, Porsche 911 Cabriolet, and new-for-1980 Mercedes-Benz SL being obvious examples. The smallest, most specialist manufacturers also enjoyed success in the sports car scene, with models like the oh-so-traditional Morgan 4/4 and Plus 8, new-generation TVR 400/420/450 Convertibles, Maserati Biturbo Spider, and vintage-looking Panther Kallista all helping to keep the market alive, if not exactly kicking. Sales figures were minuscule by global standards, but at least the genre wasn't completely dead. In fact, it was simply having a bit of a nap in preparation for the onslaught that was to come.

ABOVE Full convertible versions of the classic Porsche 911 proved popular with wealthy buyers throughout the 1980s. *(Porsche)*

RIGHT Those who appreciated retro looks but who didn't fancy a Morgan could always opt for a Panther Kallista instead – still an interesting used buy today. *(Author)*

RIGHT Some much-loved sports cars did make it successfully through the '80s, including the Alfa Romeo Spider, which by then was being built by Pininfarina. *(Alfa Romeo)*

EUNOS
ROADSTER

Back with a **bang**

To say the sports car returned with a vengeance at the end of the 1980s and on into the 1990s would be something of an understatement. And it was largely thanks to the Japanese that such a dramatic turnaround took place.

Much of the credit can be laid fairly and squarely at the door of Mazda, a company with a generally unexciting range of models (the rotary-engined RX-7 being the obvious exception) prior to 1989. But then, on 9 February that year, at the Chicago Motor Show, Mazda unveiled the most important new sports car in decades: the utterly brilliant MX-5. Here was a traditional two-seater, rear-wheel-drive, soft-top sportster that harked back to the glory days of the '60s in terms of feel and layout, but which managed to blend modern-style performance, handling, and (most importantly) reliability into the mix.

It would be difficult to overstate the importance of the MX-5 and what it meant to the world's car market. Suddenly, attention was turned back towards the traditional sports car scene – and the timing couldn't have been better. By the end of the 1980s, with insurance premiums soaring and their fashionable status fading, hot hatches were no longer the must-have accessory for yuppie-types

ABOVE For a decade that saw so many classic sports cars killed off, its final year saw one of the most vital sports car launches of all time: the first Mazda MX-5 of 1989. *(Mazda)*

ABOVE The resurrection of the Lotus Elan name in 1989 was a reasonable success, though the design and tooling ended up being eventually sold to Kia. *(Kia)*

RIGHT V8 power and awesome performance only partly hid the fact that the MG RV8 was little more than a rehashed MGB. *(MG Rover)*

everywhere. Thanks to the superb efforts of Mazda's engineers and marketing people, the sports car was top dog once again.

What was it that made the MX-5 so special? Certainly not its adventurous technical specification, for mechanically it was no more exciting than a good many family saloons and hatches of the time. But the way Mazda's development engineers had managed to combine a reliable and durable mechanical set-up with the ultimate in charisma, character, and sheer fun factor was nothing short of brilliant. Here was a sports car that, in a straight line, could be outperformed by a good many conventional models; but get the original MX-5 on the right kind of winding road, with the hood down, the 1.6-litre motor working overtime, and the grippy rear-drive handling making light of the challenge, and you were guaranteed a grin on your face the size of a minor principality.

We'll be dealing with the various generations of MX-5 elsewhere in *The Sports Car Book,* such is this model's importance to today's thriving scene. And it surely deserves such exposure. After all, with almost three-quarters of a million MX-5s produced in total at the time of writing it is without doubt the best-selling two-seater soft-top sports car of all time.

Mind you, the much-loved Mazda wasn't the only new sports car being readied for launch at the end of the '80s. Also launched in 1989 was the important new Lotus Elan, an Isuzu-powered modern-day sportster with the looks and (in turbo guise) the performance to succeed. Its career was a patchy one though, and when production ended prematurely the whole thing was sold to Kia, who relaunched it as a Korean-built, Kia-badged model – albeit not for European consumption.

The dawn of the 1990s held much promise for sports car fanatics everywhere, and throughout the closing decade of the twentieth century a whole raft of tempting new designs joined the market. MG returned to the soft-top scene with the V8-powered RV8, although in reality this was little more than a reworked MGB – and with just 2,000 examples built it was never going to set the sales charts on fire.

Of more significance was the MG*F* of 1995, a mid-engined machine that finally brought MG back to the world of up-to-the-minute sports car design. It was joined in Europe's sports car scene by the front-wheel-drive Fiat Barchetta the following year, and the second-generation MX-5 by 1998; Alfa Romeo's Spider also returned, albeit in brand new front-drive guise, and Jaguar rejoined the clan with

the introduction of the soft-top XK8. But it was the launch of the all-new Lotus Elise that really set the sports car fan's adrenalin pumping in the late 1990s, thanks to its combination of lightweight design, mid-engined layout, terrific performance, and superlative roadholding; Lotus was well and truly back on the sports car map.

As too were Germany's most successful manufacturers, with models like the BMW Z3, Audi TT Roadster, Mercedes-Benz SLK, and Porsche Boxster all taking a bow. The tide had well and truly turned in favour of the sports car, although it was fascinating to watch how different manufacturers came up with so many contrasting interpretations of the sports car brief.

ABOVE One of the most significant – and successful – sports car launches of the 1990s was the MG*F*, Britain's new mid-engined two-seater. *(MG Rover)*

BELOW The classic sporting name of Alfa Romeo Spider reappeared, albeit in front-wheel-drive guise. This good-looking newcomer proved successful throughout Europe. *(Alfa Romeo)*

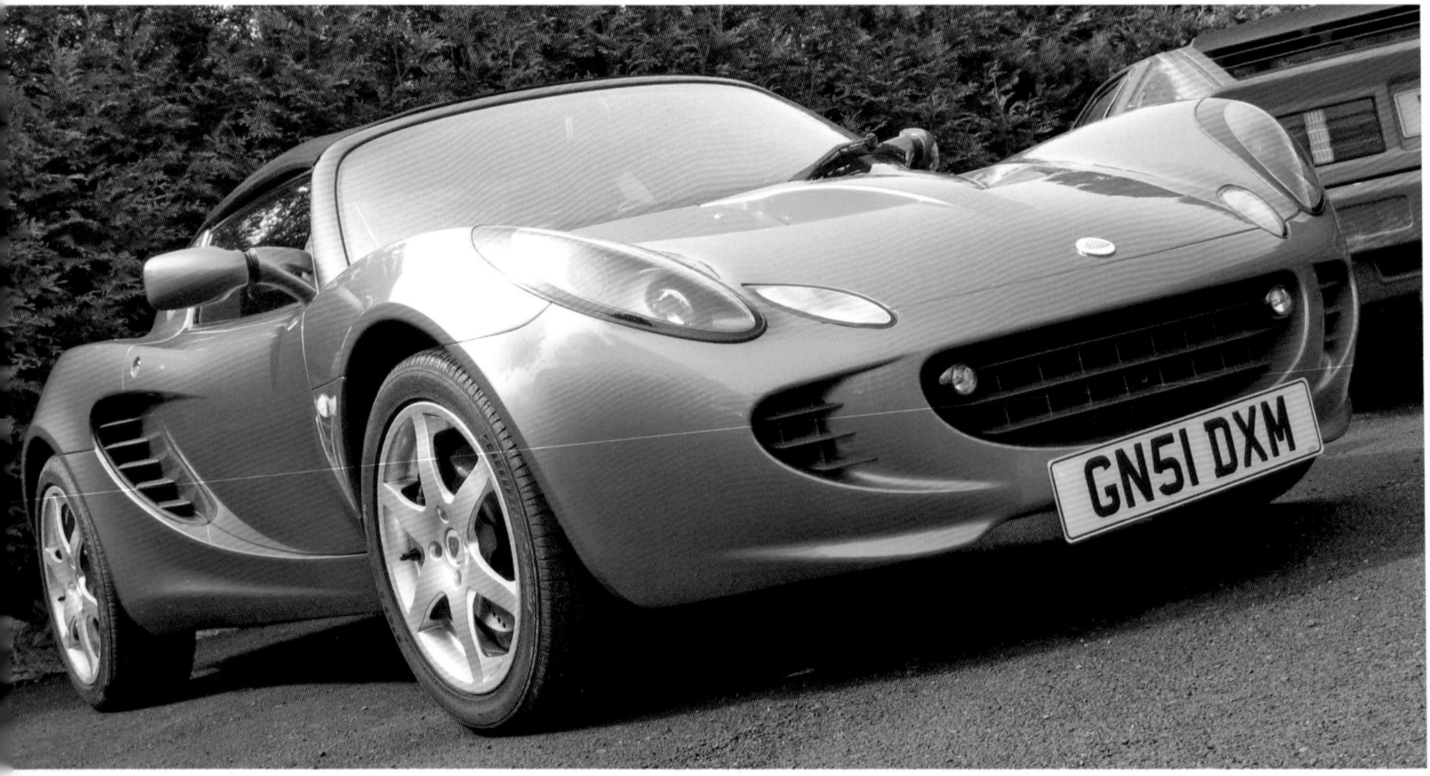
GN51 DXM

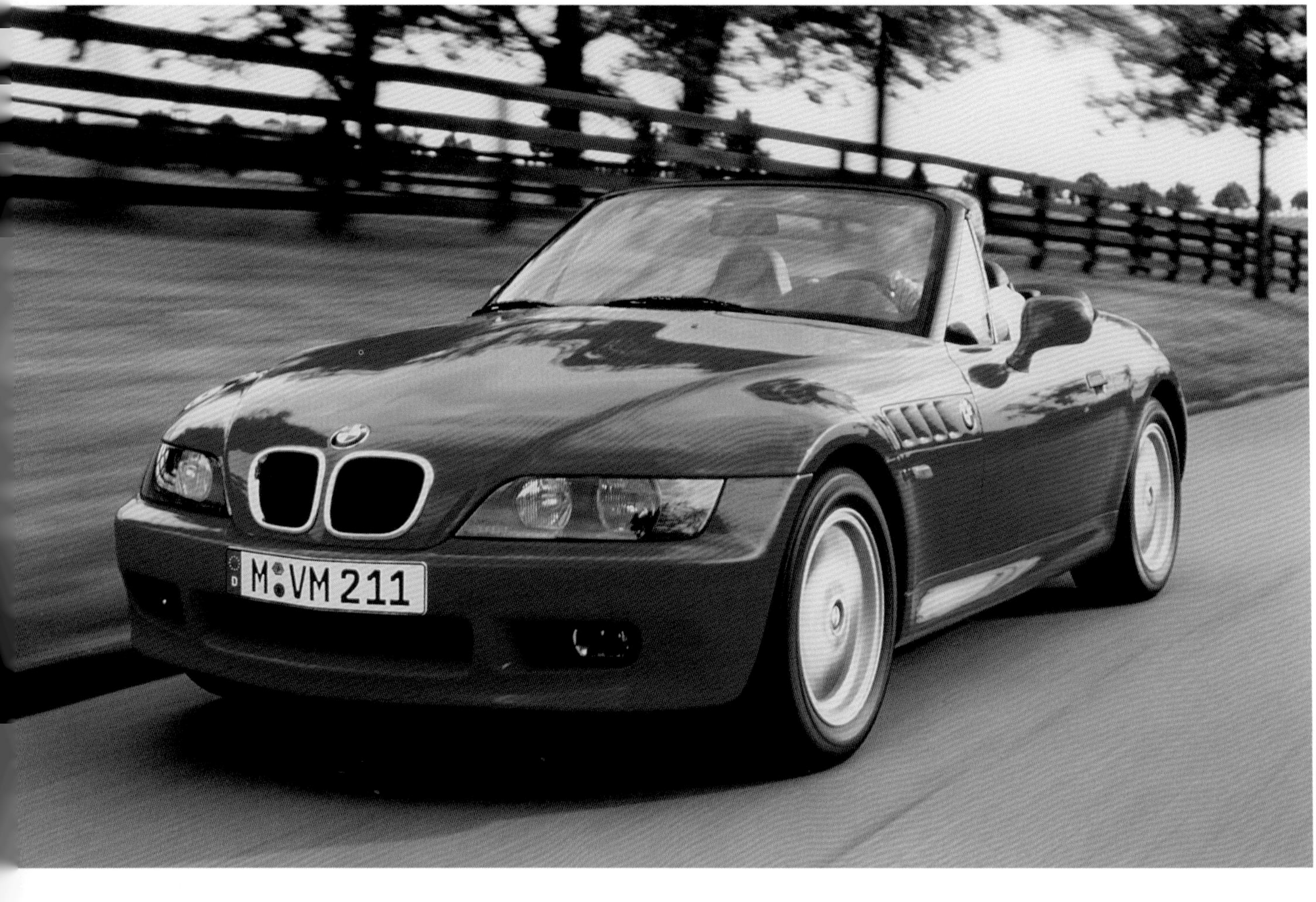
M VM 211

ABOVE LEFT It turned out to be the most successful Lotus model of all time, as well as a sporting benchmark. It's the unmistakable Elise. *(Author)*

LEFT It may not have been everyone's idea of a hedonistic sports car, but the BMW Z3 proved a popular buy throughout its lengthy life. *(BMW)*

ABOVE So popular was the first-generation Audi TT, its successor wasn't unveiled until 2005. Despite a shaky start, the TT became one of Audi's greatest success stories. *(Audi)*

BELOW For Porsche fans who couldn't afford a new 911, the arrival of the mid-engined Boxster was an event to be celebrated. Fortunately, it turned out to be a superb car in every respect. *(Porsche)*

The **new** century

Open-air motoring took off in a seriously big way in the early years of the twenty-first century, with Britain proving to be the largest market for convertibles throughout Europe. Not all of the top-down newcomers were sports cars though, with the latest Audi A4 Convertible, the metal-roofed Peugeot 206 CC, and the rather bizarre Citroën C3 Pluriel being perhaps the most obvious proof of that. For sports car fans, however, there would be some fantastically tempting machinery coming along.

Just list how many sports cars made their debut from 2000 onwards and you can't fail to be impressed. Toyota MR2 Roadster, Ford StreetKa, BMW Z4, Honda S2000, third-generation Mazda MX-5, MG TF, smart roadster, Vauxhall VX220 (better known as the Opel Speedster throughout most of Europe), Daihatsu Copen, Chrysler Crossfire, Lexus SC430, Maserati Spyder, Nissan 350Z Roadster, new-look Mercedes-Benz SLK, Morgan Aero 8, TVR Tuscan Convertible … they all appeared during the opening years of the new century. And it would be difficult to imagine a more mixed bag of performance, talent, and value for money than that little lot!

What's interesting about some of today's sports cars is how many are also available in hard-top coupé guise. It's not a new phenomenon, of course – the MGB of the 1960s could be ordered in roadster or GT (coupé) form, so it's a logical move. At the very least it enables a manufacturer to offer an extra model with minimal development costs, and fixed hard-top derivatives of the Audi TT and the Nissan 350Z, for example, have been extremely successful. For the

purposes of *The Sports Car Book,* though, we'll be leaving such versions pretty much in the background.

Such machinery makes a great buy for the right kind of enthusiast. You get the same sporty driving position, similar performance, equally impressive handling and so on. But what you don't get is the wind-in-the-hair thrills that this book insists on. It's such an intrinsic part of being a sports car owner that we reckon it's indispensable. So if you're in the market for a real sports car, forget the notion of a fixed roof. Do things properly, and we guarantee you'll end up having a lot more fun as a result. Life really can be great.

OPPOSITE Ford entered the two-seater sports car market in the twenty-first century, thanks to the launch of the cute and oh-so-fun (but short-lived) StreetKa. *(Ford)*

ABOVE Hard-top versions of sporting designs aren't generally covered in *The Sports Car Book* – unless, of course, they feature the clever folding metal roof idea found on the Lexus SC430, Daihatsu Copen, and Mercedes-Benz SLK. *(Lexus)*

LEFT Toyota's popular MR2 finally became a full convertible by the time the third-generation model arrived. The new MR2 Roadster was here. *(Toyota)*

Living
with a
sports car

Wind-in-the-hair thrills are an essential part of any sports-car experience, and one of the main attractions for enthusiasts everywhere. *(BMW)*

The **driven** wheels

Driver appeal is one of the main reasons why anybody would choose to buy a new, second-hand, or classic sports car, although head-turning good looks are never far behind on the list of priorities. Let's face it, nobody chooses to buy a Lotus Elise for its practicality or its ability to carry the shopping.

However, as the previous chapter mentioned, a sports car doesn't have to be the fastest thing on four wheels in order to be a rewarding drive.

The whole point about any sports car is that it should be fun. That doesn't necessarily mean neck-snapping acceleration, though, as often the most enjoyable sports cars have been those with charm and charisma above all else – not to mention some terrific handling characteristics.

But how do you define what makes some sports cars feel so special? Now that's tricky. It's a combination of characteristics that varies hugely between different sports cars, with much depending on a car's mechanical layout and the creativity of its overall design.

For many enthusiasts, a proper sports car has to be front-engined and rear-wheel drive (as with the Mazda MX-5 and BMW Z4), while for others only a mid-engined, rear-drive design is acceptable – as provided by the MG TF, Lotus Elise and others. Either way, the end result is a machine with a traditional sports car feel to its handling and roadholding, making for a more rewarding and more controllable experience when really pushed hard. If the rear end gets twitchy 'at the limit' with a rear-drive sportster, it's easy enough – and fun, too – to keep the revs high and use a spot of opposite-lock steering to bring the whole thing back under control, safely and quickly. For many enthusiasts, it's what sports car enjoyment is all about.

That hasn't deterred some companies from going down the front-wheel-drive route with their sports cars though, a layout that many traditionalists decry. From a manufacturing point of view, however, it makes a lot of sense. When Fiat launched its own two-seater sports car, the Barchetta, in 1996 it went the front-drive route because the newcomer was mechanically based around the Punto of the time. Using much of the Punto's underpinnings meant economies of scale during the development and manufacturing processes, which in turn enabled Fiat to offer the Barchetta in most markets at a highly competitive price.

So how did the front-wheel-drive Barchetta compare with the rear-wheel-drive Mazda MX-5 and the mid-engined MG*F* – its main competition at the time of its launch? Rather well, as far as some potential buyers were concerned. Although the Barchetta never achieved anything like the MX-5's astonishing sales success, it created its own niche following and was universally praised for its good looks, its excellent styling details, its lively performance and, yes, even its sharp handling.

You can't get away from the fact, though, that the Barchetta behaved in a very different way from its rear-wheel-drive opposition. Like most front-drive cars, it suffered from wheelspin when accelerating hard from standstill or when driven on wet or greasy roads, something that many enthusiasts couldn't take to. For the vast majority of its fans, however, the Fiat's good grip when cornering and its balanced feel were more than adequate. It also oozed character and charm, essential ingredients in its own particular sector of the sports car market. That it was only ever available in left-hand-drive guise limited its sales success in the UK and other right-hand-drive markets, but elsewhere in Europe it sold reasonably well by niche standards.

The issue of driven wheels isn't simply a choice between front- and rear-wheel drive, of course, because there are models like the Audi TT to take into consideration. In the UK in particular, the TT

OPPOSITE **OPPOSITE** Like every other BMW ever built, the front-engined Z4 employed rear-wheel drive – deemed essential by many enthusiasts. *(BMW)*

BELOW Fiat took the unusual route of making its new Barchetta two-seater a front-wheel-drive design, based as it was around Punto mechanicals. *(Fiat)*

was unique within its class for being offered solely in four-wheel-drive (quattro) guise, although elsewhere – and particularly in its native Germany – entry-level models were also offered with two-wheel drive. The TT quattro's tenacious grip and impressive handling helped maintain its reputation throughout the Series I's lengthy career, although many buyers were more concerned with its looks and image than with its ultimate road behaviour.

The TT didn't always have it its own way, with many early examples being recalled by Audi to have their suspension modified following complaints from some owners that the car was surprisingly unpredictable in certain conditions. In typical Audi style, though, the problem was addressed and the TT quattro went on to enjoy a successful career. Some enthusiasts criticised the TT quattro's almost clinical feel, its all-wheel drive being cited for its lack of character; but for large numbers of satisfied owners throughout the world, this was exactly the kind of competent, well-specced sports car they wanted.

BELOW Most fans of the Audi TT reckon four-wheel drive makes for a world-beating sports car, though front-wheel-drive versions were also available in Germany. *(Audi)*

Where's the engine?

While many enthusiasts will always opt for rear-wheel drive with their sports car, there's a school of thought that says a sportster must also be mid-engined to ensure the most fun and the best handling for your money. It's an interesting idea and, in theory, a sound one.

A mid-engined car (which basically means the power plant is positioned either directly over or ahead of the back axle) tends to offer superb weight distribution, which itself can be a major aid to handling and roadholding. And anybody who's ever driven in earnest behind the wheel of a Lotus Elise or Vauxhall VX220 will know what I'm talking about.

With a mid-engined car, there's far less rear-end breakaway when really pushed to the limit, enabling the experienced driver to tackle corners at greater speed than in a front-engined rival. And that means, whether on your favourite twisting road or exploiting your car's potential out on the track, you're making pretty rapid progress – even if, as in the case of the Lotus, your actual power

ABOVE The Lotus Elise made the MG*F* feel almost agricultural by comparison. On the other hand, the MG was the more sensible daily-use choice. Perhaps. *(Lotus)*

ABOVE When Lotus builds a mid-engined sports car, it's usually a fantastic drive. The Elise and Lotus-made Vauxhall VX220/Opel Speedster were proof of that. *(Vauxhall)*

BELOW The original MG*F* came with a mid-engined layout, yet somehow lacked the excitement and sporting edge offered by some rivals. *(MG Rover)*

output is nothing spectacular. In fact, the combination of the Elise's lightweight design and its mid-engined layout have helped ensure its reputation as one of the most fun, best-handling machines you can buy for sensible money. But not every mid-engined sports car necessarily follows the same theme.

When the all-new MG*F* was unveiled by the Rover Group in 1995, on paper at least it was one of the most exciting two-seaters in decades to wear the famous octagonal badge. Its 1.8-litre K-series engine may have been borrowed from elsewhere in the Rover line-up, but positioning it behind the driver (a first for any production MG) was guaranteed to give the new *F* real driver appeal. Or perhaps not.

While the MG*F* had a great deal going for it and soon established itself as a bestseller, it was criticised by many for its lack of sporting appeal – despite a healthy 143bhp being offered by the most powerful VVC (Variable Valve Control) version. The handling was decent enough, but the MG's Hydragas suspension wasn't the greatest set-up by mid-1990s standards and the driving position felt way too high for a sports car. The whole thing seemed to lack the charisma that MGs of old had always been renowned for, although this didn't stop the *F* from becoming extremely popular.

What's interesting about the entry level MG*F* is that the very same K-series engine in exactly the same state of tune (just 118bhp) was also used by Lotus in the Elise upon its introduction. And that made for an interesting comparison. Here we had a pair of mid-engined sports cars boasting the very same power plant, and yet the two machines couldn't have felt more different. The Elise's epoxy-bonded aluminium spaceframe-style chassis and composite bodywork resulted in a sports car that weighed in at a mere 675kg (or 1,488lb) unladen, compared with 1,073kg (2,366lb) for the MG with its conventional steel-monocoque construction.

Add into the mix the Elise's independent double-wishbone suspension (compared with the MG*F*'s Hydragas set-up) and its ultra-low driving position (a world away from the feel of sitting on an MG*F* rather than in it) and it's little wonder the two cars were so contrasting in their driving styles. The Lotus was faster, more nimble, better-handling, and a whole lot more exciting. On the other hand, it was also awkward to get in and out of, offered a soft-top that was difficult to remove and refit in a hurry, and was very much a no-compromise design in terms of its comfort and equipment levels.

The MG was a more user-friendly product, which was exactly what so many buyers of the time were demanding. It wasn't the kind of car that a track day enthusiast might choose over an Elise, but it was the kind of sportster that tens of thousands of enthusiasts were happy to use every day with no nasty surprises and little in the way of drama.

Before we leave the subject of engine positioning, of course, there's one more layout to mention – and it applies primarily to the evergreen Porsche 911, the world's only rear-engined supercar. Rear-engined sports cars have been the exception rather than the rule over the years, with only the 911 achieving cult status and a huge following. Various Karmann-Ghia vehicles of the 1960s and '70s followed the same layout, and very stylish they were, too; but as these were unashamedly based around the chassis and running gear of the classic Volkswagen Beetle, any claim of being a genuine sports car was perhaps a little tenuous.

While front-engined Porsches have come and gone over the years and have been very successful, it's inconceivable that the 911 will ever lose its rear-engined layout. It's so much a part of the car's DNA, and it's what makes it truly unique. And yet, particularly in the model's earlier days, it was as responsible for deterring many potential buyers as it was for attracting so many others.

You see, any car with its engine slung out behind the back axle is going to have 'interesting' handling characteristics. It's less of a problem on today's models, as highly sophisticated suspension designs and the availability of four-wheel drive (for the 911 Carrera 4) since the late 1980s have helped reduce the impact. But prior to this, the 911 was reviled as much as it was revered for its rather unpredictable handling characteristics.

Inexperienced 911 drivers who went into a corner too quickly and then lifted off the accelerator would be greeted with massive and unpredictable oversteer, enough to send many a novice spinning scarily out of control. Even experienced 911 owners were known to be caught out – and this from a car that churned out up to 300bhp in Turbo guise and an impressive 231bhp as a non-turbo by 1983.

BELOW How do you fancy a rear-engined sports car? The Porsche 911 caught many enthusiasts out with its unpredictable handling, but at least it was fun! *(Porsche)*

Honest approach

If two things sum up the appeal of sports cars the most, it would be their looks and their driving style, though not necessarily in that order. Aesthetics are, of course, a subjective matter, and not everyone will agree on what makes a great-looking sports car.

While some buyers will adore the distinct and dramatic appearance of a TVR Tamora (the company's entry-level offering by 2005) or the now-defunct Opel Speedster, others will prefer the more sophisticated, subtler approach of the Mazda MX-5 or Porsche Boxster. And that's fine, because it means just about every sports car ever made will have its own band of admirers, whether it's very much a niche product or a mass-market best-seller.

Surely, though, the issue of driving style is more clear-cut? I mean, a car is either great to drive or it's not ... right? Well, no. You see, no matter what the world's motoring magazines preach to their readers and no matter how much a TV programme will bang on about how thrilling one car is compared with another, everyone's definition of a good driver's car varies. And that's because different buyers have very different needs.

Before the MG TF went out of production following the collapse of MG Rover in 2005, it was seen as an ageing but worthy design. Compared with even the cheapest Lotus Elise, however, it was viewed by most motoring experts as just a tad dull. The Lotus offered greater performance, better handling and grip, oodles of character, and real thrill appeal every time you climbed behind the wheel – while the MG, by comparison, was almost boring. And yet for scores of buyers who wanted a stylish but sensible sports car that could cover high mileages each year with a modicum of comfort, reasonable refinement, and enough on-board goodies to keep most folk happy, the MG won hands down. Its driving style might not have provided the same thrills-per-mile as the Lotus, but it was easier to drive, less frantic, more relaxing, and exactly what a large proportion of pre-2005 sports car buyers demanded. And who are any of us to argue with such logic?

It's worth remembering this when deciding which sports car best suits your needs, as different pundits have different ideas of what makes a great car. It's important you're honest with yourself about exactly what you want from a sports car before you rush out and buy the nearest example that a specialist motoring magazine has been raving about. You're the one who'll be driving it, probably all year round – not the road-testers who often only experience cars for one week at a time.

So do you want a sports car that places adrenaline-pumping thrills above all else? Do you want a sports car with more refinement than your average skateboard? Do you want a sports car that's relatively sophisticated, or one that's raw and exciting? Only you can answer such questions, as only you truly understand your own lifestyle and what you expect from your next car (and probably your first sports car). Be open and honest with yourself when answering such questions, as making a mistake at this stage could prove very costly – and more than a bit upsetting – later on.

OPPOSITE Do you like your sports cars dramatic or subtle, hard or soft? Models like the no-compromise Vauxhall VX220 are a true enthusiast's dream. *(Vauxhall)*

BELOW The much underrated MG TF managed to combine a pleasing driving style with day-to-day ease of use – exactly what many buyers demanded. *(MG Rover)*

The practicalities

ABOVE The rather rare Renault Sport Spider didn't even come with a windscreen as standard equipment. Now that's what we call basic... *(Renault)*

If piloting a sports car is radically different from driving around in your average hatchback or saloon (the low-down driving position, wind-in-your-hair enjoyment and – hopefully – superior handling and roadholding guarantee that), the whole ownership experience will bring yet more contrasts. And it all starts when you stop to consider the practicalities and convenience (or otherwise) of your average sports car.

Many people with families and hectic lives do run sports cars, but these tend to be second (or maybe even third) cars. Or, in the case of the classic car scene, the kind of machinery that's kept on the road during the summer months and then tucked away in the garage to avoid the worst of the winter weather. In other words, there's usually another car (or two) that can be used for the essential things in life (school runs, shopping trips, and family holidays), leaving the sports car for the fun, carefree times when you climb behind the wheel just for the sheer hell of it.

That's logical enough. Bringing home large quantities of DIY materials from the nearest store is inevitably easier in a Mondeo Estate than in an MX-5. Having said that, however, there are plenty of owners out there who do use their sports cars as their only everyday transport, even if such folk tend to be childfree and relatively young.

Using an Opel Speedster or Lotus Elise as sole everyday transport wouldn't be straightforward for most people, not least because of these models' minuscule amount of boot space. But a sports car that has been designed with practicality high up its list of priorities (with models like the Audi TT, Mercedes-Benz SLK and Mazda MX-5 springing readily to mind) will provide as much everyday convenience as many owners will demand. In any case, wouldn't you rather be seen behind the wheel of a head-turning sports car than a terminally dull 'blandmobile' during your journey to work? As for big shopping trips … well, you could always get your stuff delivered.

To be serious, though, there's more to determining the convenience and practicality of a sports car than by simply measuring its boot space and working out how many bottles of wine you'll be able to squeeze in. For a start, just how driver-friendly is the sports car you're thinking of using every day? If you think this is a strange question, work out roughly how many times a day you clamber in and out of your car (I can guarantee, the real figure will come as a surprise) – and then try doing that with the Lotus Elise or Opel Speedster I've mentioned before. If you're anywhere near six feet tall or perhaps on the chunky side, you might be shocked by the contortionist-like positions you'll need to adopt when getting in or out of the car. And while it might be mildly amusing the first time you try it in a warm, dry showroom, the novelty could wear off after you've done it several times on a cold, wet day whilst wearing winter clothing.

'Don't be so soft,' you're probably screaming at the book by now. 'Call yourself an enthusiast? Some of us are harder than that, you know.' And that's great. Because such sensational drivers' cars deserve to be adored by petrol-headed owners who just can't get enough of them. But still, it pays to weigh up your own demands and expectations before you make any purchase. Is it everyday transport you're after, or simply a fun-a-minute track day special? The answer to that question is vital when making any sports car decision.

Finding a sports car with just the right amount of driver-friendliness for your own particular demands isn't the end of the story, though. You also need to consider, for example, where you live and what your sports car will have to encounter there. If, for instance, you have to tackle the challenge of a dozen high-riding speed humps to get to and from your house each day, you need to make sure your sports car of choice will have the ground clearance to cope. Similarly, if you live in an area with high levels of car vandalism and you have no choice but to leave your car parked in the street at night, are you wise to be choosing an attention-grabbing convertible in the first place?

ABOVE Cars like the Caterham Seven are all about driving for the sheer hell of it. *(Caterham)*

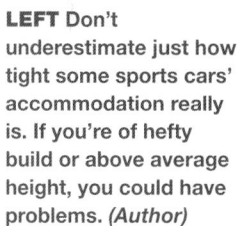

LEFT Don't underestimate just how tight some sports cars' accommodation really is. If you're of hefty build or above average height, you could have problems. *(Author)*

LEFT Now you're not going to be making many trips to the DIY store with a boot like that! A sports car for daily use needs to fit in with your own personal lifestyle. *(Author)*

LEFT The Series III was the biggest, most sophisticated, most refined MX-5 to date. And yet Mazda had cleverly retained its real fun appeal. A neat trick. *(Mazda)*

VPP 258M

Safe storage

And that brings us neatly on to the subject of storage, another important issue to bear in mind when considering the pros and cons of living with a sports car. These days, most modern cars are perfectly capable of being kept outside in just about any climate without any long-term effects. The harsh winters of Northern Europe hold no fear for most car owners, such is the reliability of today's best designs. And, in theory, a modern sports car is no exception.

Having said that, any sports car with a fabric roof that experiences such extremes of European climate as the baking summer sun of southern Spain and the heavy winter snowfall of Norway will suffer premature wear and tear to the roof itself. A new soft-top is relatively easy to have fitted on most sports cars (albeit at a price), but it's something you might need to bear in mind if your car is to be kept outside all year round.

Many of today's latest sportsters come equipped with folding metal roofs rather than fabric contraptions, of course, and theoretically this should improve the situation in the long term. That is, as long as the roof in question doesn't experience any of the functionality problems associated with certain early variations on the theme …

Storage of a new or modern sports car is relatively straightforward. If you don't have access to a garage or a carport, you keep it outside; that's that. But what if it's an elderly or classic sports car we're dealing with? Then the whole issue of storage becomes important. Keep your classic MGB or Triumph Spitfire outside in any Northern or Central European country and you'll inevitably find it leading to corrosion problems, a damp and leaky interior, pitted chromework, and much more. Even a thoroughly restored or original rust-free example will soon suffer from the ravages of winter. And it's not ideal in the hotter, more southerly countries either, where the ferocity of the summer sun can lead to 'bleached' paintwork, cracked hoods, and faded interiors.

So, garaging is the order of the day, even if that means renting garage space somewhere. It's easy enough nowadays to buy a rainproof car cover for your classic sportster, some of the more expensive ones being tailored perfectly to fit your particular make and model. But no matter how good many of these are, they're no substitute for

proper long-term storage – no cover can guarantee to keep a car completely damp-free throughout an entire winter.

Mind you, some garages aren't as dry as they should be either. Even if there are no leaks, it's possible for condensation to build up in a garage, leaving your car covered in a thin, glistening layer of damp. And if you can see that on its paintwork, you can be sure it's also covering every structural box section (inside and out). If you have mains electricity in your garage, it's worth considering buying a dehumidifier to keep the air dry throughout the damp winter months. It could do wonders for your classic's longevity.

Of course, to keep your sports car in tip-top condition there's really no substitute for getting out and about in it as often as possible. But, as the next chapter will reveal, running your own sports car isn't always plain sailing.

OPPOSITE Leaving any sports car outside all year round will have an effect on its condition. Do that with an old classic and you could really have problems… *(Author)*

BELOW Long-term storage (even in a dry garage) can cause harm. The best thing for any sports car is regular use and an enthusiastic owner… *(MG Rover)*

Running
a sports car

Most sports cars use
engines and major
componentry from
elsewhere within their
manufacturers' ranges.
The front-drive Alfa
Romeo Spider was no
exception.
(Alfa Romeo)

Component sharing

On so many levels, the cost of running and maintaining a sports car needn't be any more expensive – or any more complicated – than for a perfectly ordinary saloon or hatchback. This is because so many of today's most popular sports cars use components 'borrowed' either from elsewhere within their manufacturer's range or from another mass-market company.

Just because your sports car wears a Lotus, Morgan, or Caterham badge, for example, doesn't mean it's an over-complicated machine made up of expensive-to-maintain parts. In fact, the vast majority of its mechanical and electrical components will be straight off a shelf somewhere.

Look under the skin of an early Lotus Elise, for example, and you'll find a perfectly ordinary K-series ex-Rover engine. Glance under the bonnet of a front-wheel-drive Alfa Romeo Spider and you'll see the same 2.0-litre Twin Spark or 3.0-litre V6 used in the Alfa 156 and 166 models of the same era. And if you take a peek under most Audi TTs, you'll find the same 1.8-litre turbocharged power plant that proved so successful in the VW Golf. It's the same story with the majority of today's new, used and classic sports cars, so it pays to bear this in mind. In theory, at least, it's no more expensive to carry out an engine service on a specialist sports car than it is on a Plain Jane hatchback if both vehicles employ the same power plant.

This isn't a new phenomenon. Sports car manufacturers have always made the most of their own parts bins, as well as those of other companies keen to supply to third parties. Indeed, when MG – one of the most famous sports car names of all time – was founded in the 1920s, it offered nothing more than a modified Morris line-up. That's not surprising, as MG founder Cecil Kimber was sales manager of Morris Garages from 1921 onwards, which would eventually lead to those world-renowned initials of MG. And although MG went on to produce uniquely styled sports cars in later years, it never lost its reliance on components from its parent group.

That was true throughout the 1950s, '60s, and '70s, when the MGA boasted the same 1,622cc B-series engine that also saw good service in various Austin and Morris family saloons of the time; when the MG Midget used the same four-cylinder A-series engines that had proved so successful in the Austin A35, Morris Minor, and Austin A40 of its era; and when the good old MGB spent 18 years being powered by the same 1,798cc version of the B-series engine that went on to keep the Morris Marina and Austin 1800 chugging along. Admittedly, you'd sometimes find a twin-carburettor set-up on the sports car that you wouldn't on the saloon, but that was usually about as far as any upgrades went.

The trend didn't end with engine sharing, either. Glance under most MG Midgets and you'll find the same transmission (albeit with closer ratios), steering, and suspension systems as BMC's various small saloons of the time. Alright, so the Mk II Midget onwards came with front disc brakes, but even these were of a simple design that meant they could be interchanged with the Morris Minor and Austin A40 of the era, enabling useful braking upgrades of both saloons should their owners be interested.

Of course, with its cute, two-seater styling, its low-down driving position, and its weight-saving advantages, any MG Midget would always prove a far more enjoyable and exciting drive than any of its four-seater stablemates. And that's as it should be – these cars were all about cheap and cheerful fun behind the wheel.

For buyers of classic sports cars these days, such component sharing brings obvious advantages, not the least of which is a more plentiful supply of spares. Learn as much as you can about the interchangeability of your sports car's components with other vehicles and you'll find sourcing spares and accessories at autojumbles and via classic car specialists that much easier. The more cars it fits, the more readily available a 'new old stock' part is likely to be.

This, of course, is of little relevance to owners of new or modern sports cars, you might assume. And yet the sharing of components between various models within a manufacturer's range can bring benefits all round – no matter how old (or otherwise) your sports car might be.

OPPOSITE Glance under the bonnet of an MG Midget and you'll find the same 1,275cc engine that powered plenty of Marinas, Allegros, and Minis over the years. *(Andrew Noakes)*

BELOW The MGB's 1,798cc B-series engine was used elsewhere in the BMC and British Leyland line-ups over the years – from the Morris Marina to the Austin Princess. Like so many sports cars, they relied on components from more mass-market models in order to keep production costs realistic. *(MG Rover)*

Servicing and maintenance

You see, irrespective of whether we're talking about a specialist, low-volume model or a market-leading bestseller, using well-proven and readily accessible components from elsewhere brings obvious economies of scale.

No company as small as Lotus, Caterham, or Westfield could afford to design and produce its own engine or transmission these days, particularly given the constraints imposed by emissions and safety legislation, so buying in engines and other major components from outside makes great sense. Admittedly, TVR has been an exception to this rule at times, by producing its own power plants – but equally, this British concern also made use of other company's engines over the years, and to great effect.

So, assuming you're the proud owner of a low-volume sports car from a specialist manufacturer, what's the situation when it comes to servicing and maintenance? Don't worry, because there's plenty

OPPOSITE Thanks to it's relatively uncomplicated design, a Mazda MX-5 isn't a difficult machine to repair and maintain even on a tight budget. *(James Mann)*

LEFT Using an independent specialist rather than a franchised dealer can often save money, as well as gaining you a more enthusiastic service. *(Author)*

of choice out there, starting with the main dealer for your particular marque. Taking your Elise to an official Lotus dealership for its regular servicing will get the job done, and the costs involved shouldn't be too horrific by main dealer standards. But you might also consider using one of the many independent Lotus specialists that can be found in the UK and beyond, the kind of companies that offer spares, servicing, and repairs for all Lotus models (classic and modern) but which aren't a part of the official Lotus set-up.

The advantage might be one of cost or simply a more convenient location. Either way, many of these specialists are thriving nowadays, attracting owners who want to take advantage of their enthusiasm, dedication, and all-round knowledge. And whatever sports car you're thinking of buying, there's usually going to be a choice of independent specialists available – and that doesn't just mean for owners of low-volume models from the smallest manufacturers.

Take the world's best-selling two-seater – the Mazda MX-5 – as an obvious example. Whatever the age of your MX-5, your nearest official Mazda

dealership will be happy to service and maintain it for you. But, assuming its manufacturer's warranty has expired and you're free to shop around for a better deal, you'll find a plethora of independent MX-5 specialists only too willing to service, repair, modify, or maintain your treasured machine. And often at prices that seriously undercut those charged elsewhere.

Some owners will suggest it's worth paying the extra to ensure there's an official Mazda dealer's stamp next to every entry in your car's service record, suggesting the car could maintain its value better as a result. In reality though, this is rarely the case. When the time comes to sell your car, few buyers will be deterred by the fact that an MX-5 specialist carried out all the servicing for you rather than a franchised dealer; indeed, many potential buyers might prefer this, as it could suggest an owner who has doted on their car and ensured it has only ever been worked upon by specialists with an in-depth knowledge rather than technicians who also service the rest of the Mazda range.

Whatever make or model you're thinking of buying, you'll find the independent specialist scene has matured a great deal and – in the vast majority of cases – now offers an excellent service. Before you buy the car of your choice, carry out an Internet search to see what specialists can be found reasonably close to where you live; and why not check out some of the specialist motoring magazines or classic car titles to see which companies are advertising and who seems to offer the best service for your particular needs.

We've listed a large selection of specialists in Appendix A of this book, but no list can be fully comprehensive – so don't forget to shop around. Whether it's a classic Triumph TR6 or Morgan 4/4, a second-hand MGF or Mazda MX-5, or a nearly new Lotus Elise or smart roadster that does it for you, there are specialists around who'll be willing to both sell you a car and carry out all the maintenance and servicing afterwards.

One final thought on this subject. It pays to do your homework before you splash out on any make or model of car you've never owned before, so make sure you contact both a main dealer and an independent specialist to ask about the cost of servicing before you take the plunge. Nowadays even the smallest specialist companies often have fixed-price servicing deals available, enabling you to predict with reasonable accuracy the kind of expenditure that lies ahead. Neglect this and you might end up with bigger bills than you were expecting. It always pays to be prepared.

BELOW Finding the nearest independent specialist for your particular make or model usually means nothing more than an Internet search or a glance through a few magazines. *(Author)*

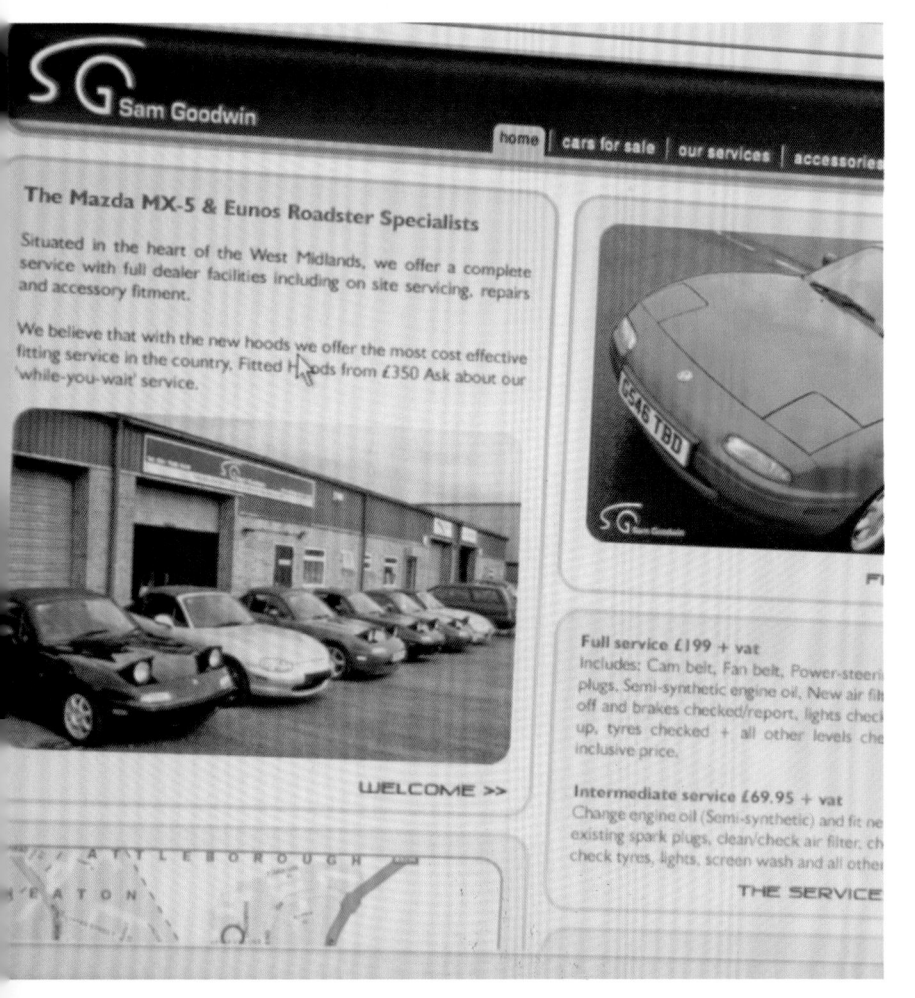

Parts and **petrol**

Many owners – particularly on today's classic car scene – prefer to do much of their own servicing and maintenance, and there's absolutely nothing wrong with that ... apart from the fact that you won't have a fully stamped service record when the time comes to sell. This is less of an issue with classic sports cars, perhaps, although it still pays to keep the receipts for every item of expenditure during your period of ownership.

On more modern vehicles, though, buyers will quite rightly expect a full service history, even if it's not an official franchised dealer that's been carrying out the services.

Those who do carry out all their own work can still benefit from the independent specialists that are out there, as the majority of these offer excellent mail order facilities for anybody needing spares and accessories. If you're lucky enough to have an independent specialist close by, of course, you can buy all the stuff you need over the counter.

Don't forget your local motor factors and car spares shops too, which can also be useful sources of parts for even the most specialist sports cars. If you're on a tight budget they'll be able to supply non-genuine items for a wide range of vehicles; so this is, again, where a working knowledge of the interchangeability of components can prove very worthwhile. Knowing what other cars a certain part fits might save you time and

ABOVE So many parts are interchangeable between your sports car and many less specialised models that it pays to do your homework before you go shopping. *(Author)*

money when going shopping. Your friendly motor factor may look blank when you ask for a set of brake pads for a classic TVR; but if you know they're exactly the same as the pads fitted to a boring mass-market saloon he might actually have some in stock.

The issue of budgets and expenditure can't be covered, of course, without at least a brief mention of fuel economy – or lack of – although the importance of this varies between individual owners. If you're buying a classic sports car in which you expect to drive just a few hundred miles each year, it's of little consequence whether you're achieving 25mpg or 35mpg. In the grand scheme of things, the difference in cost is fairly marginal. On the other hand, if you're looking for a more modern everyday machine in which you expect to drive 20,000 miles per year, the importance of fuel consumption suddenly increases.

But how does fuel consumption vary between a sports car and a similarly-engined conventional vehicle? Well, to be honest, the figures often stack up pretty well. One of today's most popular used sports cars, for example, is the MG TF, which in top-of-the-range 160 VVC guise shows an official average fuel consumption figure of 37.6mpg. Interestingly, the Rover 25-based MG ZR 160

(fitted with the same engine in the same state of tune) shows an identical official figure, despite being a very different kind of vehicle. Now, such numbers may not represent the economy you can expect in real-life driving conditions, but they serve to illustrate how a proper sports car needn't be any more expensive at the pumps than a saloon or hatch with similar power.

Another example would be a second-hand 2004-model Mazda MX-5 1.8i, a sportster with an official overall consumption figure of 32.5mpg. By comparison, a family-size Mazda 6 TS five-door (also boasting a 1.8-litre engine) offers an official figure of 36.2mpg. The difference is there, but it's not a huge margin – and most MX-5 owners would agree that it's a penalty worth paying!

Incidentally, some of today's more specialist sports cars often provide some of the biggest surprises in terms of fuel consumption, and the Lotus Elise 1.8i is no exception. With an overall official fuel consumption figure of 38.5mpg, it could be seen as positively frugal by performance car standards. Admittedly, much will depend on how you drive your Elise as to whether you'll ever get anywhere near that figure in daily use, but it's a tribute to the car's lightweight design that it manages to come up with such impressive official economy.

BELOW Official figures show identical fuel economy for both the MG TF 160 VVC and the equivalent MG ZR hot hatch. *(MG Rover)*

Insurance issues

Insurance is an obvious area of concern for many first-time sports car buyers, and understandably so. If you've only ever been used to insuring fairly low-powered family vehicles, you might assume you'll be paying a great deal more to insure a rather rapid or maybe even highly collectable sports car. And in many cases you'd be right; but there are some ways in which you can bring down the cost of your insurance, no matter what the make, model, or age of the car.

When trying to insure a modern or new sports car, it's as important as ever that you spend some time shopping around, via both telephone calls and the Internet. It makes sense to get a quote from your existing insurer, but this should be just one of many that you obtain. You could be amazed by how much the costs vary.

Personally, I've always had greater success in getting keen insurance quotes via the telephone than the Internet, as it enables the customer to stress any relevant facts that could bring down the cost. My experience might not be repeated in your case, though, so consider all options before agreeing to a particular policy. Interestingly, today's insurance policies are becoming more 'tailored' than before, so if your annual sports car mileage is likely to be very low, your car is going to be kept in a fully alarmed garage, you'll only ever drive it at weekends, you've taken part in a recognised advanced driver's scheme, you're a member of an owners' club for your model, or you have a blemish-free record of driving company cars for

ABOVE Tempted by a 'grey' import? Then you could find yourself paying extra for your insurance. It pays to check this out before you buy the car. *(Author)*

many years, mention all this and it could well have a beneficial effect on your quote.

Most potential buyers are aware these days of specialist classic car insurance, which usually offers limited-mileage agreed-value policies at highly competitive prices. Insurers know that the owner of a cherished classic sports car is likely to take greater care of it than somebody who drives a battered old Mondeo, so the risks involved are relatively low. As long as you satisfy the criteria of most classic car insurers in terms of your age and driving record, and the age, specification, and garaging arrangements of your car, you could find that the cost of insurance works out far less than you first imagined. For further details, check out the specialist insurance advertisements in any of today's classic car magazines (which, in the UK, include *Classic Car Mart*, *Practical Classics*, *Classic & Sports Car*, *Classic Cars*, and *Octane*) and give them a call for an exact quote.

More good news is that the classic car insurance industry has broadened and matured over the years, which means some of the previous rules and regulations no longer apply. At first, for example, such schemes insisted that a car had to be around 20 years of age before it could be considered a classic, which proved frustrating to many owners. Now, though, most classic car insurers will consider younger classics, while many even have their own schemes specifically for certain makes and models. These days, it's easy enough to insure an early Mazda MX-5, Lotus Elise, MG*F*, or Jaguar XK8 on a limited-mileage classic car policy, as a lot of insurers recognise the restricted use of many such vehicles as second cars. And that brings obvious cost benefits to the owners.

Finally, what's the situation if you want to insure a 'grey' sports car – in other words, a vehicle that has been imported second-hand from Japan? There are plenty of these around, with the Mazda MX-5 (often badged as a Eunos when in Japanese-spec) being among the most popular. Happily, it's easier now than it's ever been to find suitable insurance cover for such 'non-official' sports cars, with most mainstream insurance companies willing to offer cover on 'grey' MX-5s, Honda Beats, Toyota MR2s, Mitsubishi FTOs and all the other popular imports. But there is a

downside – and that means you'll find yourself paying anything between 25 and 40 per cent extra compared with the cost of insuring a UK-spec vehicle.

Why does this extra expense exist? For a variety of reasons. Certain 'grey' models, it seems, are statistically more likely to be stolen or involved in accidents than their UK-spec equivalents. (There's no obvious, logical reason for this – but since when did statistics take logic into account?) Many grey imports also tend to be better equipped and cosmetically more complicated, which means even a minor shunt can involve the replacement of more trim, trickier paint schemes and the like.

Whatever the make, model or specification of sports car you're trying to get insured, you'll find shopping around for quotes well worthwhile – but make sure you do this before you take the plunge and end up buying a vehicle that you simply can't afford to insure. Also, don't forget to give some of today's specialist sports and performance car insurers a try before automatically opting for one of the more mainstream operators; you may find a policy more suited to your needs, particularly if your vehicle is non-standard or is an unusual model. Check out any enthusiasts' car magazine to catch these performance-specialising insurance companies' latest advertisements and special offers.

OPPOSITE Even modern classics like the Jaguar XK8 can be insured on a 'classic' policy – depending, of course, on your own age, driving record, and location. *(Jaguar)*

BELOW Buying a classic sports car? Don't forget your agreed-value classic car insurance, extremely affordable thanks to its annual mileage restrictions. *(Norton Insurance)*

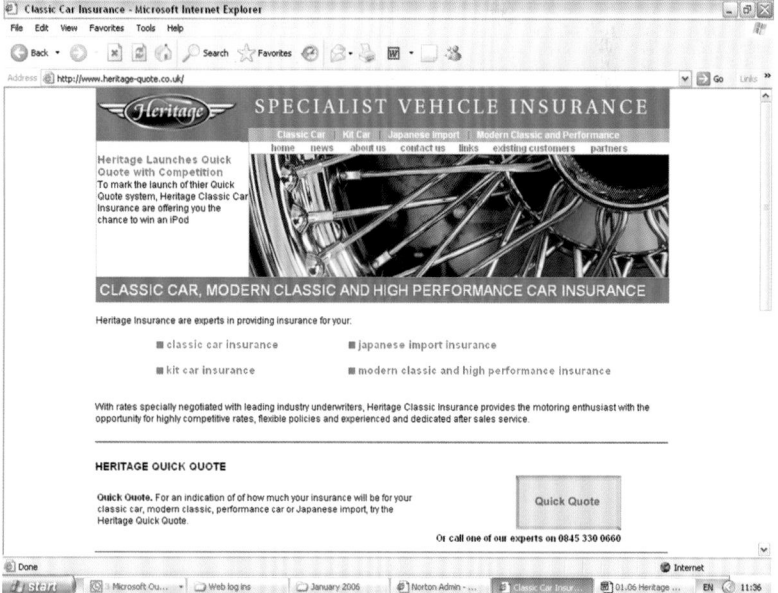

Preparing
for the MoT

Motorists' dread of the annual MoT test (compulsory for all cars over three years of age in the UK) hasn't changed much over the years, even if the test itself is now drastically different from when it was introduced at the end of the 1960s.

Back then, as long as your car stopped and steered it stood a reasonable chance of passing. Nowadays inspectors are a bit more thorough, and despite our moans and groans about the unfairness of it all, most of us would probably agree that tightening up the test was a good move in terms of public safety.

Relatively few vehicles pass their MoT tests first time every time, but you can increase the chances by spending less than a day getting your sports car ready. And with the cost of the MoT test now at an all-time high, it's wise to be prepared. Admittedly, our procedure won't guarantee a pass, but it might make you aware of problem areas before you actually venture to the local MoT garage.

First, though, a word about legalities. Despite what some prophets of doom might tell you, it *is* still legal for you to drive your car to its MoT test even if your old certificate has expired – as long as you have valid insurance cover, the MoT is pre-booked, and you drive there by the quickest route (not via your favourite holiday destination). Make sure your MoT garage has written your name and the make, model, and registration number of your car in their appointments book, though – this will then cover you should you get stopped by the police on your way there.

Now down to business: what should you be on the lookout for? First, bodywork. Generally, there should be no rot within 30cm of load-bearing metal or component mounting points. And if there's rust elsewhere, it must not pose a threat to anybody via jagged or sharp edges. With some older classic sports cars employing a sturdy separate chassis, you must also ensure that this crucial backbone of your vehicle is in good order and not showing major signs of rot.

Before the MoT test, it pays to go over your sports car's bodywork extremely carefully, on the lookout for any corrosion problems that may have started since last year. These are best dealt with now, before they become a major problem in the

LEFT Have you checked your tyres lately? Excessively worn tread or cracked sidewalls could result in an MoT failure. *(Andrew Noakes)*

future. So even if that bit of rot near the sill isn't necessarily an MoT failure item this time round, it's going to be cheaper and easier to deal with now than when it poses a threat to roadworthiness later on.

Other areas that are easy to check prior to an MoT include lighting (don't forget your number plate lights, hazard warning lights, and reversing lights), wipers, windscreen washers, and horn. Make sure all are working as they should. Also

BELOW Structural rust like this will be easily spotted by the MoT tester. The only long-term cure is to replace the entire panel – or at least the rotten section of steel. *(Author)*

check that the seat belts are securely mounted, that there's no corrosion around the seat belt mounts, and that the belts themselves are free of fraying or any other damage.

Now it's time to get your sports car on sturdy axle stands and get your hands dirty, firstly by checking out its suspension. Assuming it's a fairly traditional, straightforward set-up, ensure the dampers are free of leaks and corrosion and that you inspect all areas – including springs – for potential damage. Also check out the condition of the wheel bearings by rocking the wheels, looking for excessive lateral movement. None of these basic tests at home will be as thorough as an MoT examiner's rigorous check-over, but they'll at least give advance warning of major problem areas.

RIGHT Are you sure your sports car is ready for its MoT test? A thorough check-over beforehand will ensure it stands a better chance of passing first time. The difference between a pass and a fail can be down to something as straightforward as replacing brake pads or a suspension bush. *(James Mann)*

Moving on to the steering, check for excessive play in all the joints. As with suspension, all rubber bushes should be examined, looking for splits and signs of perishing. Look for leaks from the steering box and make sure it's securely mounted.

It's also essential that your brakes are given a thorough going over, from the levels and condition of your brake fluid (has it been changed in the last couple of years?) to the state of the shoes/pads, not forgetting to examine brake pipes and flexible hoses in the process. Also, make sure the parking brake is effective and properly adjusted.

Fluid level checks are vital before you venture out onto the road; we're talking clutch and brake fluid, engine oil (check it again the day after you change the oil), transmission and axle oils, and, where applicable, damper fluid levels. Then there's the engine coolant: is the antifreeze mix strong enough (vital even in summer, as it helps reduce corrosion) and has the coolant been drained and replaced recently?

Don't forget to check your tyres. Each must have 1.6mm of tread depth across the central 75 per cent of the tread, around the whole tyre. Look for cracked sidewalls while you're at it – an increasingly common problem and a real pain, as it can mean an MoT failure even when there's ample tread remaining. Still, it's not worth messing about, not when you can receive three penalty points per tyre on your driving licence if you're caught driving with illegal rubber.

Then, of course, there's the emissions test, an area of concern primarily for owners whose vehicle are neglected, haven't been regularly serviced, or have covered a massive mileage and are well past their best. If you care about your sports car, having it serviced at the same time its MoT is due will hopefully reduce the chances of it failing the emissions section of the test. Don't forget, however, that many older classics will only be subjected to a 'visual' test of emissions (looking for signs of excessive smoke) due to their age. Your MoT examiner will advise you on the most recent rulings regarding this.

Like other areas of this chapter, much of this MoT advice comes down to common sense, although it's often the smallest areas of preparation that get forgotten. So just because you've rebuilt the brakes and serviced the suspension on your much-loved sports car, don't assume it'll sail through a test. Just a blocked washer jet or a split windscreen wiper rubber could put a stop to that. Don't let that happen to you. Be vigilant, and there's every chance of success.

LEFT During your pre-MoT check-over, don't forget easily overlooked items like lights, horn, washers, and wipers. They're usually cheap and easy to fix. *(Author)*

BELOW If you're unsure about your pre-MoT checklist, you could always ask a few friends to give you a hand… *(Triumph)*

Brand new options

With an ancestry
dating back to 1957,
the wonderfully basic
ex-Lotus Caterham
Seven is one of the
most thrilling drives
you'll ever experience.
(Caterham)

Most affordable

If you've already decided that your next (or maybe first) venture into sports car ownership is going to involve buying a brand new example, then this is the chapter for you. There's an impressive array of models from which to choose. As ever, though, much depends on your available budget and, of course, your own particular needs and expectations.

The issue of budget will probably be uppermost in your mind, so we'll deal with that first. The cheapest proper sports cars on today's market tend to start at prices around the same as you'd pay for a fairly lowly Ford Focus or Vauxhall/Opel Astra. At the other end of the scale, you can choose to spend as much on a luxury two-seater sports car as many people might invest in a house. The health of your bank balance (or the generosity of your bank manager) will play a large part in just how many sports car choices are actually available to you.

Starting with the most affordable offerings available to those determined to buy a brand new machine, we can't ignore the evergreen Fiat Barchetta, surely one of Europe's best-value sports cars of the twenty-first century. Available only in left-hand drive (even in those countries where right-hand drive is the norm), the Barchetta has been a popular choice for several years with those seeking the most style for the least cash.

So what is it above all else that makes the Barchetta such a tempting proposition? Well, it's not the fastest sports car on the street, but neither is it a sluggard. It's fun, characterful, and competitively priced, and its glorious Italian styling simply oozes neat touches and smart detailing. It's clean looking, and yet very individual. It's not the most up-to-the-minute design you can buy, but for many people that's part of its charm. It may not follow the traditional route of rear-wheel drive, but the front-drive Barchetta still has plenty of old-school attributes.

Power comes from a 1.8-litre 16-valve four-cylinder lump, pumping out a healthy rather than outstanding 130bhp. The rev-happy nature of the engine, its decent sound quality, and its sheer eagerness (124mph, with a 0–100kmh, or 0–60mph, sprint in a far-from-disgraceful 8.9 seconds) add even more to the Barchetta's strong argument.

When pitching together the power outputs of different sports cars, by the way, it's important to compare like with like. An official figure of 130bhp for the Fiat Barchetta might not sound particularly special, but it's 8bhp more than the current entry-level Mazda MX-5 can muster – and that's a machine that, in most markets, costs a whopping 25 per cent more to buy brand new than the Italian offering.

In any case, the feel of a sports car is more important than its on-paper power and performance figures might suggest. And that's never been truer than with the oddly named Daihatsu Copen, a diminutive two-seater with an electrically-operated folding metal roof and a mere 659cc four-cylinder turbocharged motor under its

bonnet. This churns out a paltry-sounding 67bhp, which equates to a top speed of 106mph and 0–100kmh in 11.7 seconds – which, by sports car standards, is almost bordering on the sloth-like. But to dismiss the Copen purely because of this could mean you're missing out on a terrific all-round driving experience.

Many enthusiasts are finally coming round to the idea that you don't need to be driving at Gatso-busting speeds in order to have the most fun behind the wheel, with relatively recent models like the smart roadster underlining this. And the Daihatsu Copen is further proof. The styling may not be to everyone's taste (looking almost like a scaled-down Audi TT, you either love or loathe its curvaceous looks), but the way the Copen's tiny engine screams its intent and makes full use of its wide rev band gives plenty of low-rent thrills behind the wheel.

The Copen's engine sounds superb, its almost raucous note at high revs suiting perfectly the frantic nature of the thing. Extra power from the turbocharger comes in as low as 2,000rpm, which means you're able to make the most of what power is available virtually all the time. Link all that to a slick gearchange, sharp steering, and more than adequate grip and you've got a fascinating concoction of fun and entertainment.

But Cars as small as the Copen aren't for everyone, its tiny stature proving just too diminutive for many buyers. In any case, for not much more than you'd pay for the Daihatsu you could buy a brand new entry-level Caterham Seven – and that's a choice that still appeals to those buyers looking for maximum thrills with minimum frills.

OPPOSITE Looking for an affordable new sports car? They don't offer much more charm or much better value than the terrific little Fiat Barchetta. *(Fiat)*

BELOW The smallest example of open-air fun sold in Europe has to be the Daihatsu Copen, a diminutive but fun-to-drive package. *(Daihatsu)*

Extra thrills

The Caterham's ancestry goes right back to 1957, when it was launched as the Lotus Seven and built by Colin Chapman's up-and-coming sports car company. By the early '70s, though, Lotus was intending to discontinue production of the Seven, much to the consternation of Graham Nearn, who had been an official Lotus dealer since the end of the '50s.

Nearn saw a continuing market for the Seven and so bought the production rights and tooling from Lotus and set up his own factory in Caterham, England. As Lotus moved further upmarket throughout the 1970s, Nearn and his re-badged Caterham Seven (available in part-assembled or complete form, depending on your budget) went from strength to strength. After half a century of success, the Caterham (nee Lotus) Seven continues in production to this day.

Base models start in price at around what you'd pay for an entry-level family-size saloon, which means they're reasonably affordable. But what exactly do you get for your money? Well, by modern standards, not a lot. Part of the Caterham Seven's timeless appeal is its basic charm, which contributes to its ultra lightweight design and, of course, its astonishing performance potential.

Even the cheapest 1.6-litre (Ford Sigma-engined) Seven will hit 100km/h (62mph) in a mere 5.9 seconds before going on to a top speed of

112mph – despite having just 125bhp lurking under its bonnet. And with your backside only inches from the floor and your right foot making the most of the Caterham's traditional rear-drive handling and amazing grip, the whole experience feels even more rapid than that!

Most expensive Caterham Seven at the time of writing is the truly awesome 2.0-litre Duratec-engined Superlight R400, a version with 210bhp on tap and enough acceleration potential to hit 100km/h in a neck-jarring 3.8 seconds. With a 140mph top speed and a power-to-weight ratio of 420bhp per tonne, there's no other machine quite like it.

The whole point about the Caterham Seven, though, is that you don't need to spend a serious amount of money on a version like the Superlight R400 in order to have enormous fun behind the wheel. Whichever model your budget will stretch to, you can be assured one of the most exhilarating four-wheel experiences of your life. Just don't go expecting anything (and I mean anything) in the way of creature comforts, will you?

If the styling and feel of a Caterham appeals, you also have the successful Westfield range at your disposal, with the Westfield 1600i being the most affordable, undercutting the Sport 1600 and Sport 2000 models that follow. Like most Westfields, it's available in a choice of Starter Kit, Module Built or Factory Built stages, depending upon your budget and how handy you are with a

set of spanners. As with Caterham, the factory will be happy to build you a brand new, turn-key example if your finances will allow.

Amazingly, if a relatively small four-cylinder engine doesn't float your boat when it comes to sports cars, Westfield has the answer in the shape of its SEiGHT model – a version of the existing Westfield design fitted with nothing less than a 3950cc ex-Rover V8 engine pumping out 200bhp-plus. I'd suggest this is moving too far away from the original design principle of basic performance, but not everyone agrees; the SEiGHT has its own small but enthusiastic fan base. The company even offers a version of its sportster powered by a 170bhp, 1137cc Honda Blackbird motorbike engine, known as the Westfield Megabird – and, once the revs are heading towards the 10,000rpm mark, it's is a seriously quick piece of kit.

LEFT No, it's not a Caterham. The British firm of Westfield has carved itself a healthy niche of the specialist sports car market in recent years. *(Westfield)*

OPPOSITE With so much performance on tap from such a basic, lightweight package, it's no wonder the Caterham is a force to be reckoned with out on the track. *(Caterham)*

BELOW You won't find airbags or air-conditioning in a Caterham Seven! This is the closest thing you'll get to a road-going go-kart. *(Caterham)*

The MX-5 phenomenon

Still affordable on today's new-car scene, despite having been gradually shifted more upmarket with each successive new-generation model, is the latest incarnation of the evergreen Mazda MX-5, now officially the world's most successful two-seater sports car of all time.

In fact, at the time of writing no less than three-quarters of a million MX-5s have rolled down the production line, a phenomenal achievement given that the original model of 1989 was intended to be very much a niche product.

The latest generation MX-5 was unveiled to an expectant audience at the Geneva Motor Show in March 2005, the newcomer going on sale in most export markets by the autumn of that year. And the verdict? Another clever reinterpretation of the MX-5's timeless styling, this time with bulging wheel arches, a dramatic front air dam, and a new look of sophistication about the whole stance. The MX-5's DNA is recognisable even at first glance, but this time in a style far more in tune with twenty-first-century tastes.

Beneath the skin, too, new developments have arisen, most noticeable of which is a choice of 1,798cc or 1,999cc DOHC 16-valve power, the latter offering a highly useful 156bhp at 6,700rpm. Even the smaller-engined (124bhp) version boasts a top end of 122mph (196kmh), hitting 100kmh in 9.4 seconds. Opt for the 2.0-litre, though, and you'll find up to 130mph (209kmh) at your disposal, with the 100kmh sprint time reduced to just 7.9 seconds. As before, there are quicker sports cars on the market right now, but the MX-5's eager nature and all-round fun appeal means it feels faster – and is therefore far more enjoyable to pilot enthusiastically – than any official figures might suggest.

MX-5 transmission options include five- and six-speed manual or six-speed automatic, while new suspension design (double wishbone front with a multi-link rear) has resulted in even more impressive handling and roadholding to cope with the extra power.

Thanks to the clever use of ultra-high-tensile steel, the new MX-5 offers more bodyshell rigidity and strength than just about any rival, while still managing to weigh in at barely more than the Series II model of the late '90s. It means an MX-5 driving experience that's just as much fun as before, but this time with the rigidity and safety you'd expect from a modern-day design.

The MX-5 has retained its traditional front-engine, rear-wheel-drive approach even in its latest guise, and it's a layout that its many fans seem to appreciate. The car has evolved and

improved a great deal, and is now a far more sophisticated product than Mazda ever intended way back in the 1980s. But that's the way much of the sports car market has gone in the twenty-first century, and Mazda has done well to keep pace with changes in buyers' demands. Even so, there are many who seek machinery with more of a raw edge, which is where Lotus has been happy to oblige in recent years.

ABOVE The first of the third-generation MX-5s rolls off the production line back in 2005, an important moment in Mazda's history. *(Mazda)*

BELOW Better equipped, safer, more rigid, stronger – the latest MX-5 was designed with twenty-first-century buyers' demands very much in mind. *(Mazda)*

The Lotus position

If Lotus moved upmarket in the 1970s with the dropping of the Seven and the introduction of the supercar Esprit range, the Norfolk company has arguably returned to its roots in more recent times. The announcement of the all-new Elise in 1996 brought some much-needed excitement back to the Lotus brand, and the model has been a consistently strong seller ever since.

At the time of writing, the most affordable brand new Elise is the 111R, a car that's very different from the first Elise models. Gone is the original ex-Rover 1.8-litre K-series engine, replaced these days by a 1,796cc 16-valve DOHC Toyota unit with VVTL-i (Variable Valve Timing and Lift) technology. It's a far more sophisticated engine than its predecessor, and significantly more powerful too. Output is rated at 189bhp at a heady 7,800rpm, enough for a top speed of 150mph and 0–100kmh in a mere 5.2 seconds. It's exhilarating stuff.

The Elise has grown up over the years and is now better-equipped and more user-friendly compared with the stripped-out feel of the original. Back in 1996 there was no air conditioning, sound system or heater in the Elise, so things have moved on quite a bit since then. Even so, the car has lost none of its excitement or real enthusiasts' appeal, and still deserves serious consideration by anybody looking for more thrills than your average European soft-top can provide.

The Elise isn't the only model available brand new from Lotus these days, with the hard-top Exige and latest Europa S coupé also doing well for themselves. But for many, it will always be the ragtop Elise that best sums up what makes a great Lotus sports car, and the current 111R is no exception.

It's a more upmarket machine than an entry-level Elise was ever originally intended to be, but the world's sports car scene has moved on a great deal since 1996. These days, the latest mid-engined Elise – with its six-speed close-ratio gearbox, uprated springs, retuned dampers, and stronger rear subframe – goes and feels better than ever. No wonder Britain's *Autocar* magazine, in a test of the Elise 111R, claimed that it 'offers a driving experience no rival can touch for intimacy and involvement'. That's praise indeed in one of the most hotly contested sectors of today's sports car scene.

BELOW Today's Elise may be a more sophisticated product than it was back in the '90s, but it's lost none of its raw appeal or its exhilarating driving style. (Lotus)

Creature comforts

ABOVE The Chrysler Crossfire may not be the most technologically advanced sports car in its class, but it does offer excellent value on today's new-car scene. *(DaimlerChrysler)*

No matter how grown up the 111R is compared with earlier Elises, it's still a specialist machine that demands a few too many compromises for some buyers. There are other cars out there that manage to offer more refinement, comfort, and convenience than any Elise will ever manage, even if they then run the risk of feeling less exciting as a result. Still, different buyers have different needs, and the more mass-market manufacturers are only too happy to oblige.

The kind of money you could spend on an Elise 111R will also buy a brand new Honda S2000, entry-level BMW Z4, Chrysler Crossfire Roadster, Audi TT Roadster, or Nissan 350Z Convertible, any of which will provide a sophisticated and easy-to-live-with alternative to the Lotus's more raw approach. But would one of these machines satisfy your own personal shopping list of requirements?

For the true sports car enthusiast, the Chrysler Crossfire is arguably the easiest to dismiss. Based around the underpinnings of the old-generation Mercedes-Benz SLK, this distinctive-looking offering generally lacks excitement. Many will buy it because it simply looks different; others will revel in its characterful nature and its excellent value for money. But anybody expecting a nerve-tingling experience from the entry-level 3.2-litre Crossfire Roadster could be in for a disappointment.

The Mercedes-Benz V6 engine is a decent unit, linked to either five-speed automatic or six-speed manual transmission. And with 215bhp available, it should be quite a thrill, especially as it hits 100kmh from standstill in just seven seconds. But with fairly soft suspension and steering that seems to lack precision and feedback, it's not the most rewarding drive on the new-car market.

For even better performance, you could spend around 30 per cent extra on the Crossfire SRT-6 Roadster, fitted with a supercharged version of the same V6, this time with a massive 330bhp on tap, equating to 250kmh (155mph) flat out, hitting 100kmh from rest in just 5.5 seconds. That's impressive performance for the price, although the Crossfire's handsome looks are spoiled somewhat by the SRT-6's bizarre looking add-ons and spoilers.

The Crossfire's mixed bag of talent prompted Britain's *Autocar* magazine to suggest that 'the Roadster is not the enthusiast's choice because it is very little fun to drive, but then buyers in the target market may not be doing that'. And maybe that's what BMW was also assuming with the launch of the Z4 range, a massive improvement over its predecessor (the Z3) but still not what many people think of as an enthusiasts' sports car.

That, of course, doesn't stop the Z4 from being a huge sales success, aided by its wide choice of models, the allure of its BMW badge, its fantastic build quality, its excellent residuals and, of course, its sheer good looks. Depending on your budget and your preferences, you'll get 2.0-, 2.5-, or 3.0-litre power, ranging from 167 to 231bhp, not to mention a choice of 'base', SE, or Sport specification levels.

The cheapest Z4 2.0i undercuts the Chrysler Crossfire in most markets, while the top-of-the-range 3.0si Sport is roughly on a par price-wise with the SRT-6 mentioned earlier. There's little doubt that, in almost every respect, the Z4 is the superior machine, although not every motoring pundit is full of compliments. *Car* magazine's summary of the range was 'Save up and buy a Boxster', while *Autocar* suggested that 'it's still not as involving as some of us would like'. Mind you, they did conclude that the Z4 is 'the logical place to put £27k if you find an Elise too hardcore'.

Another logical place for such cash – and another desirable new sports car bearing a German badge – is the latest Audi TT Roadster, a clever reinvention of the big-selling original. It still looks like a TT but, dynamically, is a vital step forward.

There was nothing intrinsically wrong with the first-generation TT. In quattro guise, it became a top-handling, strong performing, great-looking model that proved impressively popular in almost every market it entered. By 2006, though, it was

growing old and needed a freshen-up – which arrived in the shape of the bigger, better, latest-generation TT.

Like its predecessor, this version is available in hard- and soft-top guises, though it's the Roadster version we're particularly interested in here. As before there's a choice of four-cylinder turbo or 3.2-litre normally-aspirated six-cylinder power, the latter churning out a rather decent 250bhp. And with quattro all-wheel-drive handling to match, this is by any standards a worthy successor to the much-loved 'old' model.

The latest TT's bigger dimensions and improved design have created a sports car with

ABOVE At the heart of the Crossfire sits a Mercedes-Benz V6 unit, with outputs ranging from 215 to 330bhp. *(DaimlerChrysler)*

BELOW The BMW Z4 was seen as a major advance over its predecessor, the Z3. It's still easy to appreciate its overall appeal. *(BMW)*

ABOVE The Z4's styling was very much in tune with BMW's twenty-first-century corporate look, helping it to stand out from its upmarket sports car competition. *(BMW)*

BELOW Replacing such an icon as the first-generation TT wasn't easy. Audi came up trumps in 2006, though, when the Series II TT Roadster was finally unveiled. *(Audi)*

more space, more convenience, and more comfort than before. And if such considerations are important to you, it's a superb choice, whichever model falls within your budget. But for more great thrills at similar (or less) money, it's worth looking in the general direction of Japan.

Turning **Japanese**

Ah yes, the Honda S2000. If you think the S2000 is just like any other civilised sports car, think again. This is a machine that likes to be thrashed in order to make the most of its capabilities. That's because its maximum power of 237bhp isn't developed until a motorbike-like 8,300rpm, although the engine will spin freely right up to 9,000rpm before the rev limiter brings things back under control.

And compared with some of the more user-friendly, boulevard-cruising convertibles out there, that makes the Honda a bit of a monster.

Not only is this a powerful engine, it also sounds fantastic. The VTEC four-cylinder screams like a banshee when it's near the limit, giving the S2000 driver the kind of aural thrills that would delight any airline pilot. And with this amazing engine linked to a super-slick, extremely fast, six-speed gearchange, you're able to make rapid progress indeed. In fact, the S2000 will reach in excess of 240kmh (150mph), with 100kmh coming up in a mere 6.2 seconds.

This car isn't just about straight-line performance, though. Honda invested a great deal of time, energy, and hard cash into ensuring the new S2000 was an impressive handler – and it paid off handsomely. Britain's *Auto Express* magazine praised the Honda for its 'perfect weight distribution and sharp, precise handling', going on

ABOVE Beneath the S2000's handsome bodyshell sat a gem of an engine, churning out 237bhp – and all without the aid of a turbocharger. *(Honda)*

RIGHT Lowering yourself into the S2000's driver's seat and heading for the tarmac for the first time is guaranteed to be an exhilarating experience. *(Honda)*

BELOW Chopping the roof off the standard 350Z Coupé created Nissan's new Roadster, one of the best-looking convertibles to come out of Japan in recent times. *(Nissan)*

to describe its cornering as 'predictable and fun'.

The fact that the S2000 boasts a rear-drive chassis gives it the feel of a 'proper' sports car, but Honda weren't about to leave it at that. The S2000 features an extremely low centre of gravity, 50/50 weight distribution, and an engine mounted well behind the front axle. These three crucial factors are complemented by the immensely rigid bodyshell, which means that the age-old convertible problem of scuttle shake is now a thing of the past. This is a remarkable machine by any standards.

As is its fellow countryman, the Nissan 350Z Roadster, long-awaited soft-top version of the highly successful 350Z Coupé. And with the same 276bhp V6 power plant, six-speed super-slick transmission, and grin-inducing handling as its hard-top brother, the Roadster makes a hugely tempting choice in this sector of the market.

The power of the 350Z makes its presence felt as soon as you lower yourself into the driver's seat and fire up the fabulous V6 that lies ahead of you. Maximum output is generated at 6,200rpm, which means lots of adrenalin-pumping action when you make the most of this rev-happy engine's playful nature.

The engine itself is situated well back in the 350Z – a substantial way behind the front axle, in fact, leading Nissan to describe it as 'front/mid-mounted'. That helps to explain the 350's impressive 53/47 per cent front-to-rear weight distribution, aided by a particularly low centre of

gravity. No wonder this machine is among the top-handling soft-top sports cars at its price level.

What the 350Z Coupé and Roadster have both achieved is to bring respect and desirability back to Nissan Z-car line-up at long last, providing the world with an up-to-the-minute design with unmistakeable aesthetic overtones of the original 240Z. This was one of the most exciting things to happen to the Nissan line-up in a very long time – and it worked brilliantly. Not only is the 350Z selling strongly in every export market it enters, it is also surely destined for future classic status. Z-car fanatics are suddenly very happy people once again.

ABOVE With Japanese levels of build quality and standard equipment, the 350Z proves tempting for more than just its superb on-road behaviour. *(Nissan)*

BELOW The 350Z's near-perfect weight distribution helps to create one of the top handling roadsters in its class It's good to see Nissan's Z-car legend back on form. *(Nissan)*

Upmarket
offerings

If a prestigious German badge is what you crave most for your next brand new sports car, there are some great options out there in addition to the Audi TT and BMW Z4 we've already covered. In fact, with a selection of open-top offerings available between them, Mercedes-Benz and Porsche know a thing or two about the upmarket sports car.

Cheapest of the Mercedes sportsters is the latest-spec SLK, the second-generation version launched in 2004 and a useful improvement over the hugely popular previous model. It's more expensive than the car it replaced, but the latest SLK is a superb offering – and far more sporting than old-style SLK drivers were ever used to. In fact, at long last the Mercedes SLK is a genuine sports car that any enthusiast could enjoy.

It's better looking than it used to be, thanks to its curvaceous, sexier styling that seems to ooze attitude. It boasts the same kind of clever folding metal roof mechanism, but now with more space on board and a better-equipped interior.

Under the bonnet things get really interesting. The smallest power plant is the familiar 1.8-litre supercharged unit, developing 161bhp and powering the entry-level SLK 200 Kompressor. Further up the range, though, you have a choice of 2.8- or 3.5-litre V6 propulsion, thanks to the 228bhp SLK 280 and 268bhp SLK 350 respectively. And then there's the outrageous, range-topping SLK 55 AMG, a 5.4-litre eight-cylinder behemoth with a massive 355bhp of raw power on tap.

Driving the latest SLK is a far cry from what's gone before, with even the smallest-engined version boasting a 143mph (230kmh) top speed and 0–100kmh in less than eight seconds. The SLK 350, by contrast, achieves 155mph (250kmh) and takes just 5.5 seconds to reach 100kmh, with superb handling and grip and genuine sports car thrills adding further weight to its argument.

Two more convertible Mercedes-Benz models are offered, though the four-seater CLK Cabriolet could never be called a sports car – and nor was it ever meant to be. But what about the awesomely expensive SL range? Here's a classic in its own lifetime, the latest versions of which are dearer, more opulent, and more desirable than ever before.

The range starts with the entry-level, V6-engined, 245bhp SL350 (which costs more than two SLK 200Ks put together), and climaxes with the SL65 AMG, a 612bhp monster that's pricier than your average detached house in many countries. But is today's Mercedes SL really a proper sports car or (AMG versions aside) more of a boulevard cruiser?

Well, this most upmarket of Mercedes convertibles has all the power, performance, and driver appeal of any sports car, albeit wrapped up in a luxury package that's almost unrivalled on today's scene. If that's what you're looking for and you have the means to afford it, you'll find it an astonishingly capable machine.

As is another of Germany's most upmarket open-top sports cars, the Porsche 911 Cabriolet. This convertible version of the long-running rear-engined supercar starts at roughly similar price levels to the most affordable Mercedes SL. That buys you a 3.6-litre, 325bhp version of the 997-series Carrera Cabriolet, although those with an even bigger budget can get as much as 450bhp from their (996-series) open-air 911 thanks to the availability of the Turbo S Cabriolet.

While most 911 buyers opt for classic coupé styling, there's a steady demand for the hood-down thrills of the Cabriolet, and it remains one of the world's most desirable sports cars – as well as one of the most expensive, which is where the mid-engined Porsche Boxster suddenly becomes an interesting alternative.

Cynics have suggested in the past that the only reason somebody buys a Boxster is because they can't afford a 911; but to suggest that is to do the car a disservice. You see, the original Boxster was always an impressive machine, and the second-generation latest-spec model is even better.

Costing roughly half what you'd pay for the least expensive 911 Cabriolet in most markets, the cheapest Boxster is powered by a 2.7-litre six-cylinder 'Boxer' engine pumping out a very healthy 240bhp. But for those who demand even more power, the Boxster S is the perfect choice, its 3.2-litre version of the same engine seeing 280bhp with ease, equating to a top speed of 268kmh (166mph) and 0–100kmh in an amazing 5.5 seconds.

ABOVE Now that's serious sophistication! The iconic Mercedes-Benz SL-class gets even better – and even more expensive – with each new version. *(DaimlerChrysler)*

BELOW Porsche 911 Convertibles have a long lineage and a large fan base. Latest versions are faster, more refined, and more foolproof than ever before. *(Porsche)*

RIGHT The current Porsche 911 Turbo ranks as one of the most powerful convertibles on today's market, with up to 450bhp available from the rear-mounted engine. *(Porsche)*

BELOW A seriously accomplished sports car can be yours in the shape of the latest Porsche Boxster, with a choice of 2.7- or 3.2-litre 'Boxer' power. *(Porsche)*

Such figures compare well with any other sports car of similar price, but there's far more to the latest Boxster than sheer straight-line performance. There's also its fantastic driver appeal, with tenacious grip, flat handling, super-sharp steering, and glorious six-speed manual transmission (a far better choice than the semi-automatic Tiptronic S version) adding to the mix. This car delivers more feedback and response than almost anything else in its class, and by any standards it's a phenomenal machine. Make no mistake: you buy a Boxster for its capabilities, not just because it's massively cheaper than a 911.

Back to the **Brits**

If Germanic excellence isn't what you're seeking, however, there are other great options in the prestige market, with the latest Jaguar XK Convertible being just one. This 4.2-litre stunner is, again, a major step forward from its ageing predecessor, and has succeeded in bringing some much needed interest back to the sporting Jaguar line-up.

It's better looking, better built, and far better to drive than the original XK8, and it's a worthwhile buy for anybody otherwise tempted by an entry-level Porsche 911. It's arguably less of an enthusiasts' car than the Porsche, but the XK still offers its own impressive list of attributes.

As does its cousin, the latest Aston Martin DB9 Volante, surely one of the world's most desirable soft-top sports cars – as you'd expect, given its price position near the top end of the Mercedes SL sector. Described by Aston Martin as 'one of the most structurally rigid and best handling convertibles in the world', the DB9 Volante should be high on the shopping list of any premiership footballer.

But you don't need to spend anywhere near that much if you want a specialist British open-top sports car, as the enduring appeal of the Morgan line-up proves. These days you can choose from the 1.8-litre 4/4, the 2.0-litre Plus 4, and the 3.0-litre V6-engined Roadster (all of which retain

ABOVE Instantly recognisable as a Jaguar even at a glance, the new-for-2006 XK Convertible is still considered one of the finest upmarket offerings of today. *(Jaguar)*

BELOW For the ultimate in British sports car opulence, the Aston Martin DB9 Volante offers ragtop heaven for those with the necessary funds. *(Aston Martin)*

BOTTOM While the classic Morgan Plus 8 has now been usurped, the similarly nostalgic 4/4 range continues, with 3.0-litre V6 power available at its top end. *(Morgan)*

RIGHT It created a stir when it first appeared in 2001, but the daringly styled Morgan Aero 8 is an impressive drive, largely thanks to its ex-BMW V8 power source. *(Morgan)*

BELOW RIGHT TVR's financial woes hit an all-time low at the end of 2006, with the closure of its British factory. At the time of writing, it is expected that future TVR-badged sports cars will be built elsewhere in Europe. *(TVR)*

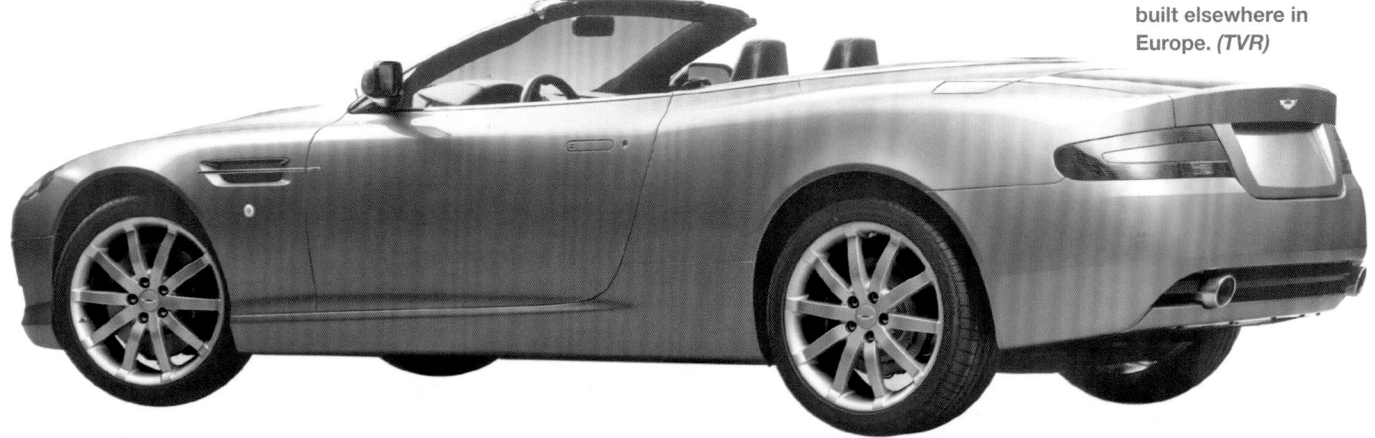

Morgan's timeless classic styling), as well as the very distinctive and vastly more contemporary (albeit with a retro twist) Aero 8, a 4.4-litre BMW-powered super-Morgan.

Too quirky? Then maybe TVR's line-up might be of interest, with the Tamora and Tuscan convertibles being the two rag-top models available up until the end of 2006. Sadly, however, all was not well as this book went to press; following the announcement of the closure of its UK-based factory, TVR went into administration soon afterwards and its future looked uncertain.

It's likely that TVR-badged sports cars will reappear on our roads (albeit built elsewhere in

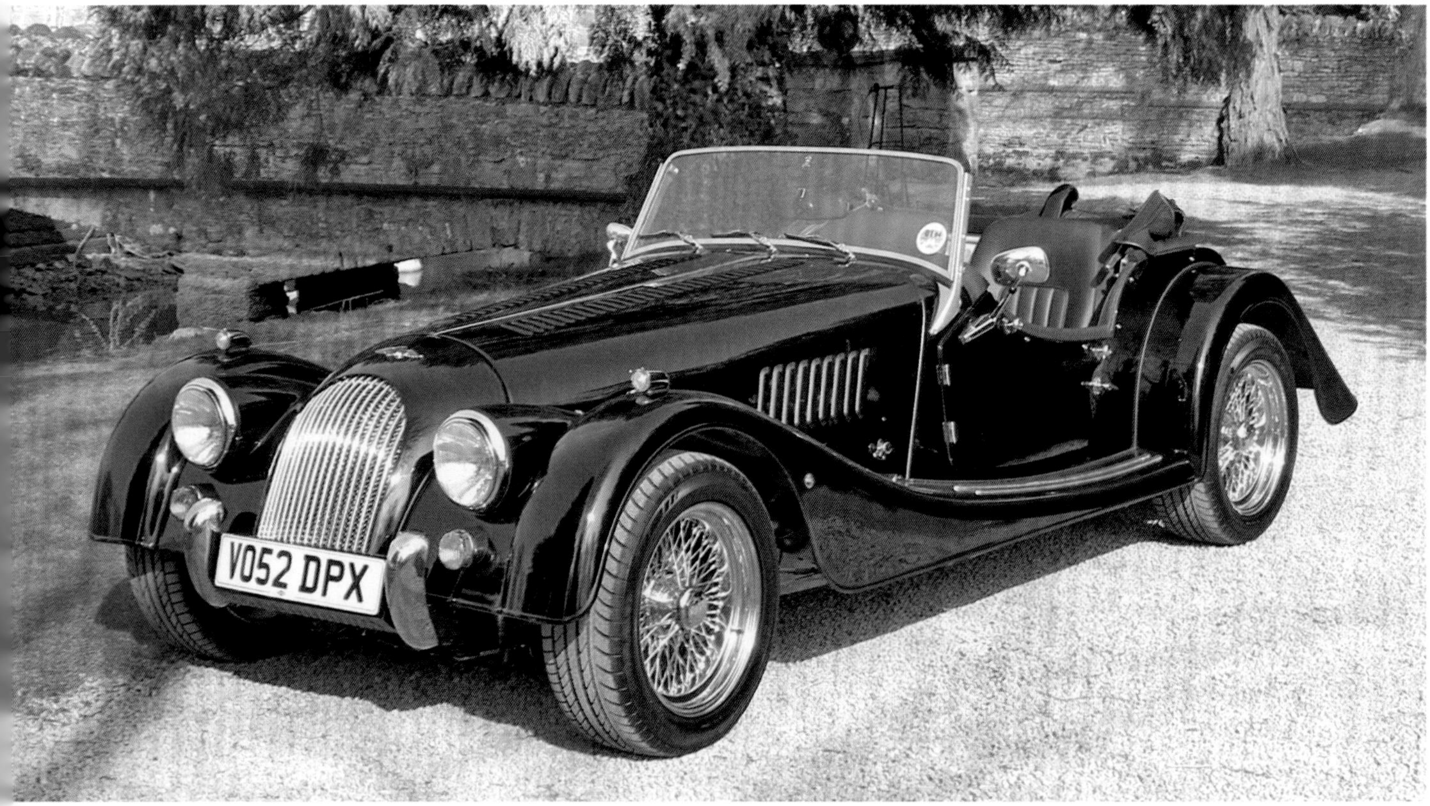

Europe), though exactly what the future line-up will be isn't certain at present.

What a shame these events have been, for even TVR's entry-level Tamora was a hugely desirable machine. Its 160mph-plus (258kmh) top speed and 0–100kmh time of just 5.5 seconds made this one of the most exciting two-seater convertibles of its time, as well as being a no-compromise antidote to mass-produced monotony. A brand new TVR may not have been to everyone's taste, but surely there are enough buyers out there to guarantee the brand's future via a new model range? By the time you're reading this, we may know a great deal more.

LEFT You'll find little in the way of modern-day sophistication aboard most new TVRs, but that's exactly how their fans love them. *(TVR)*

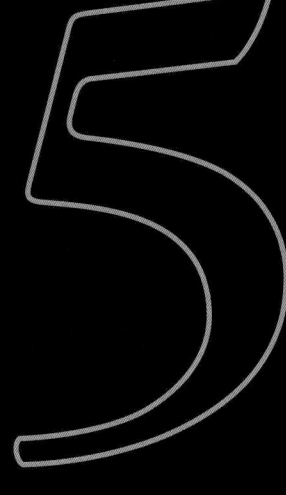

Buying
a new
sports car

**There's more to buying
a brand new sports car
than you might think.
Do you really know
about its depreciation
levels, for example?
(Audi)**

Shopping **around**

If the previous chapter has you convinced that a brand new sports car is the order of the day, there are other decisions to be made besides which model to choose. Where, for example, should you buy your car? Are new-car supermarkets useful for sports car buyers? How can you negotiate a discount? What are the golden rules when taking a test drive? And how can you keep to a minimum that most exorbitant of new-car costs – depreciation?

It's a fact that where you buy your car from will affect not only the type you buy but also the level of service that you receive. So it's as important to consider where to buy as it is to decide which make and model to choose.

In the UK and throughout most of Europe, it's the official main dealers that still supply the most new sports cars, with the majority of buyers swayed by the thought of greater service, better after-sales back-up, and an easier life should anything go wrong. A franchised dealer may have higher sticker prices – those you see on the windscreen – than a car supermarket, but in most cases there's nothing to stop you haggling to get a good discount. This depends on the make and model of car you're interested in, of course, and we'll come to the subject of haggling a little further on.

Some buyers prefer the more imaginative approach of buying through Internet-based retailers and independent brokers, and usually this allows you to quickly search and find the best prices on a wide range of cars. However, just because an independent brokerage has advertised a car doesn't mean that they'll be able to supply one quickly; quite often the wait for delivery can be much longer than when buying through an official dealership, which might make any money saved seem less worthwhile.

The UK market in particular boasts many independent new-car supermarkets, offering a huge number of makes and models covering most of the popular brands. So if it's a new Ford Focus that takes your fancy, you could be laughing all the way to the bank. For sports car buyers, though, car supermarkets aren't necessarily such good news.

Many car supermarkets do carry stock of the more mainstream sportsters from time to time, which means you might be lucky and see a discounted Mazda MX-5; but if you're interested in a more specialist model like a Lotus Elise, you stand little chance of being successful. The whole point of a car supermarket is that it buys large numbers of mass-market, easy-to-sell vehicles and offloads them to buyers, usually with very little profit per unit. It's the old 'Pile 'em High, Sell 'em Cheap' philosophy where the key is a fast turnover and a large number of sales – and that's not something that's particularly applicable to today's diverse sports car market.

Independent new-car importers were once big news in the UK, at a time when car prices were substantially higher than most of those elsewhere in Europe. Since 2000, though, UK prices have gradually become more aligned with those in other European countries, so the appeal of using an independent importer has diminished. It's still possible to save money by going through an importer, depending on currency exchange rates at the time, but don't assume that this will always be the case, as anybody who's mastered the art of haggling can often secure just as good a deal in Britain.

BELOW If the idea of buying your brand-new sportster from a car supermarket appeals, you might be disappointed to discover that most such companies specialise in more mainstream models. Still, if you're lucky you might just find an example of one of the more popular sports cars lurking at a discounted price. *(Mazda)*

Dealing with the showrooms

New-car supermarkets leave very little room for price negotiation, as their screen prices are already as keen as they can be. So for those who don't enjoy bargaining and haggling, it's a straightforward procedure of selecting your car, agreeing to pay the screen price, and arranging the financial side of things. What could be simpler?

Assuming you're buying your sports car from an official dealership for the marque, however, you need to be on your guard and be prepared to use your powers of persuasion to get the best deal.

Let's face it, as soon as you walk into a showroom you've entered the salesmen's world. They will want to be in control and guide you towards the car that they want to sell. Keep your wits about you and keep to your agenda; you know the exact sports car you want and you need to stick to this if you're to avoid being coaxed into 'upgrading' to a more expensive version.

Listen to what the salesman has to say, but don't be talked into accepting something that you don't want. A common sales trick, for example, is to try to intimidate customers, so don't allow yourself to get bullied into committing to a model or specification that's not ideal for you. Sooner or later, you'll have to talk money and you may find yourself being persuaded to spend more than you originally wanted to. The answer? If you have a budget, stick to it. Make sure you're the one in control of the negotiating.

The **price** you pay

Ah yes, negotiating. Or haggling. Or bartering. Call it what you will, being prepared to persuade any salesman to lower a car's purchase price is time well spent – and it needn't be as intimidating as many people assume.

Before you head to the showroom, you'll have researched the list price of the brand new sports car you're interested in buying. If you're in the UK, it's also worth checking out magazines like *What Car?* that give an indication of the kind of discounts you can expect on most models. If you're interested in buying a sportster with a list price of £19,000, for example, and *What Car?* suggests you should pay no more than £18,000, this gives you an idea of what to expect in that particular instance. Note, though, that the discount available off most sports cars is considerably less than you can expect off a mainstream family hatchback – and the motor trade is fully aware of this.

Car magazines don't know it all, however, and there's a chance you might be able to do even better than they suggest. For example, if you're negotiating to buy a sports car on a freezing cold, dark afternoon just before Christmas, you'll probably achieve a greater discount than if it's a scorching midsummer day when demand is far

ABOVE Researching the kind of discount levels you can expect with your new sports car will be a major aid when you head for the showrooms. *(Author)*

ABOVE Buying a brand-new specialist sports car is nothing like popping down to your nearest Ford dealer and snapping up a heavily discounted Fiesta. When it comes to the Caterhams and Morgans of this world, the list price is the price you'll end up paying. *(Caterham)*

BELOW Discount levels vary hugely. You should get some off the price of a new Crossfire, but don't expect the kind of reductions you'd have from a mass-market saloon. *(DaimlerChrysler)*

greater. Also, don't use your car-mag-trump-card too soon – you might end up showing the salesman that he should give you £1,000 off the price when, if pushed, he'd actually have been willing to go as far as a £1,500.

Be realistic when opening negotiations. Make the salesman a silly offer for a brand new sportster in his showroom and you'll lose his respect and almost certainly walk away with a poorer deal than you otherwise might have. Start from a low point (but not stupidly low) and be prepared to compromise somewhere between that and the official list price. Keep the haggling light-hearted

but make sure the salesman is aware you're willing to settle a deal there and then; if he knows you're serious, he'll be far more willing to compromise than if he thinks you're one of the 'I'll go away and think about it' brigade.

Discounts on brand new sports cars vary hugely, usually dependent on the supply and demand situation, as well as how much pressure a salesman is under to hit his target for that month. Buy a brand new Morgan and you'll be paying list price for the privilege; opt for a new Chrysler Crossfire or Audi TT, though, and you could see some flexibility.

Taking a **test** drive

Before you even start to negotiate on price, however, you need to take a few test drives to satisfy yourself as to which make and model to opt for. And, as with every other aspect of the buying process, there are some golden rules to remember when arranging new car test drives.

It's all very well kicking tyres on a forecourt or shopping in the showroom but that's no substitute for actually getting behind the wheel. A test drive is a vital part of the decision-making process, particularly when it comes to sports cars – you should never even consider buying a sportster

without having driven it. I mean, just because a couple of car magazines have raved about the model you've ordered doesn't mean that it's ideal for you or even that you'll like it.

If you're considering buying one of several makes and models, try to test-drive such sports cars back to back, or with the smallest gap between drives. It's difficult to remember how one car compares with the last if you drive them two weeks apart.

Don't be afraid to go back for a second test drive; if your dealer is serious about selling you the car, he won't object to this. Make this an extended test drive, too – a dealership will probably resist, but push for at least a half-hour drive if you can, covering a variety of different road types. Most sportsters are marketed as 'drivers' cars', so only by trying it on a selection of different roads and in varying conditions can you satisfy yourself that it's the car for you.

ABOVE Taking a test drive in the new sportster you're thinking of buying? Make sure it's more than just a quick trip to the end of the road and back. *(Porsche)*

The depreciation
trap

Choosing the ideal new sports car isn't just down to driving style, though. You obviously need to take running costs into account too, and by far the most expensive of today's motoring expenses is depreciation. This applies as much to sports cars as it does to hatchbacks, estates, SUVs, 4x4s and the like.

Happily, though, many sports cars offer well above average residual rates, which can only be good news for anybody spending their own money on a new vehicle. Even so, you still need to carry out your own research to ascertain which new sports cars hold their value best at the time you're planning to buy. The results can vary significantly.

Most new-car magazines list the estimated depreciation rates of all models, with Britain's *What Car?*, *Car*, and *Test Drive* being no exception. This makes comparing the residual values of competitive models very easy to do, and it can make for fascinating reading. In 2006, for example, *What Car?* estimated that a brand new Mazda MX-5 2.0i Sport would retain 58 per cent of its new-car list price after three years and 30,000 miles. That in itself was an excellent result when compared with various family cars that struggle to retain much more than one-third of their original price. But most buyers might think that opting for a less 'mainstream' sportster from a specialist manufacturer might bring even better results.

Well, that's not necessarily the case. The same magazine predicted that just about any version of the Lotus Elise of the same age and mileage would offer exactly the same 58 per cent residual figure as the Mazda.

So which models boast superior residuals to that? According to *What Car?*, the admittedly more expensive Nissan 350Z Convertible would retain 60 per cent of its new-car value after three years; the Mercedes-Benz SLK 280 managed a whopping 71 per cent; and the Porsche Boxster 3.2S was only a fraction behind on an impressive 70 per cent. By contrast, the cheeky little Fiat Barchetta was lagging behind in the depreciation stakes with a three-year residual value of only 45 per cent. Even that, though, was an impressive figure compared with most of the mainstream models aimed at company car users and family buyers.

The fact that you're choosing a brand new sports car instead of a more commonplace type of vehicle means you're starting to fight back at the potentially exorbitant cost of depreciation. But you can't have it all ways, as the very sports cars which retain their values most successfully are also the ones on which it's very difficult to negotiate any kind of discount.

No matter how relatively little your new car is likely to depreciate, however, it's still something that should be considered very carefully. For a sports car to lose just 30 per cent of its value in three years is superb; but if that sports car cost £35,000 to buy in the first place, you're looking at a cool overall loss of £10,500 (or £3,500 per year) in depreciation alone. Only you can decide whether that overall cost is worthwhile.

So what's the best way of truly minimising the cost of depreciation? One option is to consider buying a 12-month-old sports car that will already have taken a depreciation hit. It's a fact that the biggest annual percentage loss occurs in the first year, so this is certainly a tempting option. But there will always be people out there for whom nothing less than brand new will do. And it's a good job too, because they're the ones keeping today's sports car industry alive and well.

The **big day**

When the big day arrives and your brand new sports car is ready for collection, you'll want to pick it up with the minimum amount of hassle. However, if you get complacent or you rush things you could end up regretting it, so check your car carefully at the dealership to makes sure all is as it should be.

BELOW Collecting your brand new sports car means giving it a good check-over, looking for paintwork damage, minor dents, and even misaligned panels. If in doubt, get it fixed before you accept the car. *(DaimlerChrysler)*

Arrive on time and thoroughly inspect the car inside and out before you hand over any money or complete any paperwork. Oh, and although this may sound obvious, don't try to do a thorough inspection in the dark or wet – you won't spot any paintwork problems under such circumstances.

When inspecting the car, walk around it to check all the corners, and look carefully along its flanks to spot any minor dents or other damage. It's by no means unusual for cars to get damaged en route to the dealership or even at the garage itself, so it's vital you check thoroughly at this stage. Once you've driven away, it's easy for the dealer to claim the damage occurred after you took over custodianship. Check too that the car is exactly as specified and that all the options you expected are present and correct. The same applies to accessories: if any of the ones you ordered are missing, make sure this is sorted before you hand over your payment.

Don't forget to make sure that the pre-delivery inspection (PDI) has also been carried out and that the service record book is stamped to reflect this. After all, it's a vital part of your new car's future service history.

So, what next? Quite simply, go out and enjoy your brand new sports car. Whatever the make and model you chose, now's the time to get out there and make the most of it. Have fun!

▌ Paying the price

Paying for your brand new sports car isn't necessarily as straightforward as you might think. Of course, if you're in the fortunate position of having the funds already available, it's simply a case of presenting your supplying dealer with a banker's draft (or even your debit card) – and nothing could be easier than that. But for most buyers, there's usually some kind of loan or finance involved, which is where things can get rather more complicated.

These days, financial institutions are more eager than ever to provide car loans – which means that as long as you've got a reasonable credit rating and you can afford the monthly repayments, you should have little trouble securing a loan.

Many buyers use their existing banks for arranging loans, and obviously there's nothing wrong with that in principle. But by shopping around and spending some time both on the phone and trawling the Internet, you might be able to do a lot better when it comes to interest rates. There's so much competition around these days, lenders often have special offers available that bring down their interest rates and obviously reduce the total cost of your loan. Half a day spent researching this could save you a serious sum of money.

Do bear in mind, too, that interest rates will vary even within the same company depending upon the amount of money you're intending to borrow and, of course, your financial background. Generally, the bigger the loan is, the lower the interest rate – but, again, investigate this before you sign any agreement.

If your credit rating is poor, there may well still be companies willing to lend money for a new car – the kind of lenders who promise they'll provide you with funds no matter what your personal history is like. Sounds tempting? Maybe. But for the privilege, you could well end up paying three times as much interest as somebody with a healthier credit rating securing a loan through more conventional sources.

Finally, when you're negotiating the price of your brand-new sports car with any franchised dealer, don't forget to enquire about finance via the dealership. Manufacturers often provide their own finance schemes that can undercut the High

Street banks on interest rates – so it's worth checking out. Remember, too, that any dealership arranging finance on your behalf will be paid a healthy commission for this by the finance company – and so arranging finance through the supplying dealer could be a good bargaining point when haggling over the price of the car itself.

ABOVE You've got a brand new sportster on your drive, so what happens now? Get out there and enjoy yourself, is the obvious answer. *(Caterham)*

LEFT Looking for a loan to help finance your new sports car? There are always plenty of competitive deals on the market, so it pays to spend time shopping around and seeing what special offers are available. Don't forget the option of finance via your franchised dealer. *(Author)*

6
Second-hand sector

Merely second-hand, or a classic? The Series II MX-5 is increasingly accepted as a modern classic nowadays. *(Mazda)*

Financial priorities

ABOVE Your second-hand budget could find itself with such diverse machinery as a used BMW Z3 or a nearly new Daihatsu Copen available for similar money. (BMW)

Some of the sports cars that you might think fall into the used-car category will be dealt with in Chapter Eight, simply because they've reached a stage where they're generally considered to be modern classics rather than merely second-hand.

So if a Series I Mazda MX-5, MG*F*, or front-wheel-drive Lotus Elan appeals to you, we reckon they're now worthy of the 'up and coming classic' tag and are mentioned elsewhere. On the other hand, if a Series II MX-5, MG TF, or Lotus Elise is your thing, this is the chapter for you!

Whatever the size of your budget, you might be surprised by the number of used sports cars that – theoretically at least – are within your financial grasp. But narrowing down your choice can be fairly easy (at least to begin with) once you start looking deeper than purchase price alone. You might find, for example, that your reasonably healthy budget brings such tempting second-hand machinery as a six-year-old Audi TT 1.8T Roadster, a one-year-old Daihatsu Copen, a three-year-old Mazda MX-5 1.8i, or a five-year-old BMW Z3 2.2 Sport to your personal shopping list. That's a pretty diverse foursome, each vehicle offering its own individual attributes and appeal – but which one represents the best value?

That's more of a subjective matter than you might think, and the eventual answer depends once again on what you demand from your used car. The Daihatsu, for example, will still have two years left to run on its original manufacturer's warranty and therefore represents a particularly safe bet in terms of reliability and unexpected expense; on the other hand, it's likely to lose more in value over the next couple of years than any of the other three sportsters, as these are slightly older to begin with and have already experienced their heavier initial depreciation. This is where your own priorities come into play.

Look at servicing costs too. You could, for example, spend the same amount on a smart late-model Jaguar XJ-S Convertible as you would on a decent Series II MX-5 – but if it's an everyday car you're after, does that really make sense? The Jaguar will be less economical on fuel, potentially more expensive to service, and is likely to require more regular maintenance than the MX-5. On the other hand, if it's an occasional-use-only classic you're after, one that will grace your garage far more than the highway, the Jaguar could be a good long-term proposition.

Most **popular?**

If the Mazda MX-5 is the world's best-selling two-seater sports car of all time (which it is), it's logical to assume that the 1998–2005 Series II version is one of the most popular used choices. And with values of the earliest examples at seriously affordable levels these days, such status is justified.

Coming up with a replacement for the iconic Series I MX-5 was a tough call for Mazda. I mean, how do you replace a virtual legend? Happily for enthusiasts everywhere, the Series II model – despite being bigger and more refined – lost none of its predecessor's fun appeal, retaining its traditional front-engine-rear-drive layout and superb dynamics. The new MX-5 may have looked quite different (the pop-up headlamps disappeared, for example), but it was still recognisable as an MX-5 even with all its badges removed – and that was a clever (and vital) trick.

Any used Series II MX-5 in good order and sensibly priced will make a decent purchase now, thanks to its inherent reliability, reasonable running costs, and genuine driver appeal. There were plenty of special-edition MX-5s launched over the years too, offering extra equipment and a tad more luxury; don't be tempted, however, to pay much more for these than a standard model, as they're not exactly scarce.

ABOVE Many MX-5s on the used market are 'limited edition' models, such as this Arctic hardtop special. Be careful not to pay over the odds when buying second-hand. *(Mazda)*

ABOVE There's no shortage of used Audi TTs on today's market, though you might have to look harder if you want a scarcer version – like this 3.2-litre quattro. *(Audi)*

Scarcity is hardly a word you could use to describe the first-generation (1996–2005) Audi TT range either, with the Roadster versions being of particular interest here. Like the Mazda, these are among today's most popular open-top used sports cars, which is hardly surprising. With all-wheel drive (in quattro spec) coupled with excellent performance from the most popular 1.8-litre turbo versions, these well built and extremely reliable offerings from Germany deserve serious consideration. And thanks to such a long production run, there's a Series I TT Roadster to suit most budgets and tastes in today's used market.

Surely, though, there's more to choosing a used car than sheer popularity? Just because a particular make and model has a huge following, that doesn't automatically make it the car for you – or does it? With this in mind, we've compiled a list of our top 20 used sports cars. They're in no particular order, and they're by no means the only second-hand sportsters you might like to consider. But they are all worthy of consideration, and all have something to offer today's enthusiastic buyer. Some of them you'll already have read about in Chapter Four, where we took a look at brand new sports cars. This time round, though, we're coming at them solely from the second-hand angle. And in many cases that means fantastic value for money.

MG: THE MARQUE THAT REFUSED TO DIE

To say that the MG brand has had its fair share of ups and down over the last three decades would be an understatement.

Neglected throughout the 1970s, the Midget and MGB finally bit the dust in 1979 and '80 respectively. Two years later, though, the MG name was brought back from the dead with the launch of the MG Metro hatchback, followed over the next couple of years by the MG Maestro and MG Montego ranges. At least the famous octagonal badge was back in circulation, even if there was no proper sports car in sight.

That arrived in 1992 with the hand-built, limited edition MG RV8, paving the way for the mid-engined MG*F* in '95. The *F* was developed into TF six years later, a model that sold well until the collapse of MG Rover in April 2005 – and the subsequent sale of all the company's assets.

These days, MG is owned by Chinese group Nanjing – and, at the time of writing, there are assurances that the TF will be back in production at Britain's Longbridge plant in 2007. By the time you read this, we'll hopefully all know a lot more about what the future truly holds for the MG brand.

Second-hand options

Caterham Seven

The most raw, most hedonistic sports car available for sensible money, a second-hand Caterham makes huge sense as long as you don't want creature comforts or refinement. This no-frills machine is all about ultimate thrills, neck-snapping performance, and the most entertaining handling on four wheels – and it's strictly for the uncompromising enthusiast.

It's been around for so long that it's hard to imagine the planet without the Caterham Seven. Which means that, despite being a very specialised product, there are plenty of used examples to choose from. The best advice? Check out the manufacturer's official website (www.caterham.co.uk) and snap up a pre-owned Caterham Seven for the price of a very ordinary family hatchback. There's always a good selection available.

Fiat Barchetta

This was one of the best-value two-seater sports cars when it was new, so on the used market the little Barchetta is simply sensational. It's been around a while now, but the age-old Italian problem of premature rusting seems to have been

ABOVE When it comes to locating a secondhand Caterham Seven – one of the most fun things on four wheels – the manufacturer's website is a good place to start. *(Caterham)*

ABOVE Attractive, affordable, and terrific fun, the much-underrated Fiat Barchetta deserves consideration if you fancy something scarcer than a second-hand MX-5. *(Fiat)*

BELOW Particularly if it's a 160 VVC version you're considering, you'll find the MG TF a usefully capable and quick machine. The wood veneer trim of this example may not be to all tastes, but the interior of any TF is a comfortable and well-equipped place to find yourself. *(MG Rover)*

sorted. That's great news, because, although the soft-top Fiat might not offer the same ultimate quality as a German or Japanese sportster, it's pretty well put together and proves reliable in daily use.

Who could resist that oh-so-sweet styling, those pop-out door handles, that seriously neat hard cover for the hood when it's lowered? This is such a well thought out sports car that it's a crying shame it was always overshadowed by the MX-5. Still, that at least makes it very cheap by Mazda standards, as well as refreshingly distinctive. Not to be missed.

MG TF

Considering the TF's roots lay in the rather aged MGF, its competence came as a bit of a shock when it first took a bow in 2001. The 1.8-litre

K-series engine was pretty much as before, now with outputs ranging from 115 to 158bhp, but in every other respect the TF was a massive step forward from its predecessor.

Out went the old Hydragas suspension and in came a new coil-sprung set-up, usefully firm and neatly in tune with the TF's mid-engined layout. It resulted in an MG that not only handled better than any before it, but was also seriously good fun at any speed – at long last. The TF may have gone into hibernation with the collapse of MG Rover in 2005 (before reappearing in 2007, thanks to new owners Nanjing), but don't underestimate its relevance on the used market.

Alfa Romeo Spider

No, not the classic rear-wheel-drive Spider mentioned in Chapter Eight. We're talking here about the front-drive sportster of the same name, launched in the late '90s as sister model to the GTV hardtop coupé.

Best feature? Undoubtedly the 2.0-litre Twin Spark and 3.0-litre (later upgraded to 3.2-litre) V6 engines, either of which provides lusty performance and a superb soundtrack. And the worst? The amount of scuttle shake caused by a general lack of rigidity over bumps and potholes.

Still, that does little to spoil the driving enjoyment, thanks to the 3.0-litre's 218bhp, entertaining handling, and impressive roadholding. Plenty of wheelspin, but what a thrilling drive. Not the best-built car in its class, but surely a classic of the future?

ABOVE When the new front-wheel-drive Spider was finally unveiled, it created genuine excitement among sports car enthusiasts. Its success was assured. *(Alfa Romeo)*

LEFT A late-life minor restyle helped to keep the Spider looking fresh and modern. Choosing V6 power meant up to 3.2-litres and 225bhp. *(Alfa Romeo)*

Jaguar XK8 Convertible

The long-awaited replacement for the XJ-S finally arrived in 1996 and lasted almost a decade – which means the earliest examples are now fairly affordable. Base models offered 290bhp, increased to 300bhp when the 4.2-litre versions arrived in 2001. Fastest of the lot, though, is the 387–400bhp XKR, a supercharged behemoth capable of covering vast mileages at very high speed with barely a murmur. Grand Tourer or genuine sports car? Well, it's both.

With effortless V8 power, surprisingly competent handling, and impressive quality in its favour, any first-generation XK8 or XKR now makes an excellent used buy. Reliability is far better than Jaguars of old, though servicing and maintenance costs won't come cheap if you're on a budget. Spend the money, though – it's well worth it.

Toyota MR2 Roadster

Toyota's legendary MR2 was finally transformed into a full convertible when the all-new MR2 Roadster went on sale in 2000 – and not before time. In its latest guise, the MR2 retained its predecessor's mid-engined layout, but this time with drastically improved handling and roadholding. In fact, any second-hand MR2 Roadster is among the most entertaining cars you'll find for the money.

138bhp from a 1.8-litre power plant may not sound exciting, but the MR2 Roadster's Variable Valve Technology and relatively lightweight design means performance is well up to standard. Add terrific handling, sharp steering, and (from 2002) a close-ratio six-speed gearbox into the mix and you've got a very tempting argument for a second-

ABOVE Finally replacing the aged XJ-S, the new Jaguar XK8 of 1996 proved a steady sales success over almost a decade of production. *(Jaguar)*

RIGHT How traditionally British is that? Well, it wouldn't be a Jaguar without the obligatory 'wood and leather' look. *(Jaguar)*

ABOVE RIGHT Updates and enhancements kept the MR2 Roadster competitive throughout its life. Buy a used one now, confident in its ability to impress and entertain. *(Toyota)*

FAR RIGHT It's been said before, but the Audi TT Roadster is justifiably one of the most popular used sports cars on today's market. It's hard to argue with the logic of it. *(Audi)*

hand MR2. Just as reassuring is Toyota's reputation for class-leading reliability – so buy with confidence!

Audi TT Roadster

The first-generation TT may have had its critics over the years, but it also enjoyed a huge following worldwide – and justifiably so. Finally replaced in 2006, the original TT Roadster was a top-selling sports car for seven years and still has a large fan base today. Not surprising really, as it makes a cracking good used buy.

While front-drive entry-level models were available in Germany, some export markets (UK included) enjoyed only the all-wheel-drive quattro versions, with power ranging from a 1.8-litre turbo (180–225bhp) to – eventually – a 3.2-litre, 250bhp V6. Whichever version you choose, you'll find it a fast and competent drive, albeit slightly clinical compared with most characterful Italian sportsters.

ABOVE A second-hand Series II MX-5 not only makes financial sense but is guaranteed to impress with its on-road behaviour. (*Mazda*)

BELOW Not the most imaginative sports car interior ever created, but at least Mazda knows how to build a car well. The MX-5's overall quality has always excelled. (*Mazda*)

No matter, because the reliable and durable TT Roadster is one of the best places to spend your used-car budget. Most existing owners love them.

Mazda MX-5 Series II

The 1998–2005 second-generation MX-5 continued where the original left off, bringing traditional sports car entertainment to buyers bored with characterless motoring. Bigger and more powerful than before, the latest MX-5 was just as much fun to pilot at speed – and just as sensible to own.

The Series II MX-5 is a sensational second-hand buy, offering all the reliability and ease of ownership you'd expect. It's also more comfortable, more refined, and more practical than its predecessor as an everyday car. It's one of the best-buy used sports cars out there, with early examples now very affordable.

With 1.6- (110bhp) or 1.8-litre (146bhp) engines, any second-generation MX-5 is quick enough for most buyers' needs. Mind you, you don't need to be going fast to be having a whole lot of fun. Honestly.

BMW Z3

Hairdresser's special or genuine sports car? Opinion is divided, though much depends on which version of the Z3 you're talking about. The entry-level 1.9-litre 8-valve may have offered just 118bhp, but the 2.2- and 3.0-litre versions boasted 170 and 231bhp respectively. Then there was the awe-inspiring performance of the 325bhp Z3M …

If you want a well-built, not unattractive, extremely usable two-seater for your used-car budget, any Z3 will do the job well. But if performance is a major priority, you need to be looking at the higher-spec versions. And with depreciation levels relatively low, you might think there are better-value used sportsters out there.

For BMW fans, the Z3 is a logical and pleasing choice. And as a long-term proposition it

makes sense, too – which, in the second-hand sector, is crucial.

Porsche Boxster

Another German product that holds its value well, so even the earliest Porsche Boxster isn't exactly a giveaway. If you can afford one, though, you'll find it an absolute joy, with strong performance and some of the best handling and cornering this side of an express train. Even the entry-level 2.7-litre Boxster boasted 220bhp, enough for real fun-factor performance. For ultimate thrills, though, the 252bhp 3.2S could be worth stretching your budget for.

Critics reckon the Boxster is only bought by those who can't afford a 911, but we reckon it's much, much better than that. The Series I went out of production in 2004, and any decent example now makes a superb used buy. Reliable, beautifully built, and seriously good fun – what could be better than that?

Honda S2000

It might not be a common sight on the used market, but that doesn't mean the S2000 isn't

ABOVE The entry-level 1.9-litre Z3 may not have been particularly powerful, but to criticise the whole range for that would be to do BMW a disservice. *(BMW)*

BELOW Series I or II? The choice will depend on your budget, though just about any well cared for Porsche Boxster makes a seriously worthwhile second-hand buy. *(Porsche)*

RIGHT It's been around since 1999, yet the Honda S2000 is still a relatively unusual sight in some countries. Such exclusivity simply adds to its all-round appeal. *(Honda)*

FAR RIGHT The first mass-produced sports car to use an electrically operated folding metal roof, the original SLK was equally impressive for its all-round driver appeal. *(DaimlerChrysler)*

BELOW While early examples of the Elise offered just 118bhp, later Toyota-powered versions were a major improvement. Performance has always been excellent, thanks to Lotus's lightweight design. *(Author)*

worth seeking out. This handsome sportster arrived on the scene back in 1999 and immediately impressed with its astonishing engine and superlative handling.

Under the bonnet of this rear-drive roadster sits the most powerful normally-aspirated 2.0-litre production engine of its time, a 237bhp gem that achieves its maximum power at a heady 8,300rpm. It was all thanks to Honda's amazing achievements with VTEC (Variable Valve Timing and Lift Electronic Control) technology, resulting in an engine virtually without compare.

The S2000's cracking good handling and super-slick six-speed transmission added to its driver appeal. And Honda's legendary reliability and quality of engineering make it even more tempting as a used buy. Don't you agree?

Lotus Elise

Just 118bhp from a Lotus? That seemed woefully underpowered when the all-new Elise took a bow in 1996. But when you looked at the rest of the spec of this ultra-lightweight machine, you realised it was destined for fantastic performance potential. And as soon as you took to the wheel, you knew the Elise was one of the most exciting compact sports cars ever to appear.

It changed a lot during its first ten years on sale, with the original ex-Rover engine being replaced by a Toyota unit and the styling being dramatically updated. But the same principles of lightweight composite bodywork, mid-mounted engine, and super-firm suspension remained throughout.

This is a no-compromise sportster, lacking in creature comforts and refinement. But that's no criticism. As a raw, thrills-a-plenty fun car it remains one of today's most desirable second-hand choices.

Mercedes-Benz SLK Series I

Mercedes-style open-top motoring took on a whole new compact look in the late '90s when the Series I SLK range was unveiled, a line-up of sharply-styled roadsters featuring a clever (and now commonplace) folding metal roof design. It made other convertibles of the time suddenly seem rather archaic.

The SLK was never cheap, even in entry-level 200K guise. But then, this 163bhp supercharged version was a pretty impressive piece of kit, beaten only by the 197bhp 230K and the 218bhp SLK320. Residuals have always been strong, though the arrival of the Series II SLK in 2004 finally saw its predecessor becoming more affordable on the used market.

As sports cars go, this one's well built, refined, reliable, sophisticated, and simple to drive. If that's what you want, the SLK's a worthy choice.

TVR

Why haven't we narrowed down the choice of relatively recent TVRs to just a single model? Okay, we'll come clean: it's because just about any second-hand TVR ranks as one of the most exciting sports car buys around, even if build

BELOW Tempted by a second-hand TVR? Models like the Griffith Convertible offer an interesting niche choice in today's used market. *(TVR)*

ABOVE With a three-cylinder rear-mounted engine and paddle-shift semi-automatic transmission, the smart roadster could hardly be accused of predictability! *(DaimlerChrysler)*

BELOW Badged in the UK as a Vauxhall and in the rest of Europe as an Opel, the VX220/Speedster was heavily based on the Lotus Elise of the time. *(Vauxhall)*

quality and reliability aren't exactly up to Japanese standards. And that's why we're suggesting that, when it comes top raw thrills, a used TVR Chimaera, Griffith, Tuscan, Tamora, or Cerbera is massively tempting.

Most exciting and best value? Probably a used Chimaera, its ex-Rover V8 engine giving it serious performance and more thrills than the world's biggest rollercoaster. And with up to 320bhp available from the 5.0-litre version, you'll be hitting 62mph (100kmh) in just over four seconds whilst on your way to 167mph (268kmh) flat out. Awesome stuff.

These no-nonsense cut-price supercars are only for the very brave, both in terms of driving style and long-term durability. But if that's you, then

owning a second-hand TVR has to be on your list of things to do before you die.

smart roadster

A sports car with a 698cc three-cylinder engine and just 80bhp at its disposal? That'll be the smart roadster, one of the most hilarious, most entertaining four-wheeled devices that sensible money can buy second-hand. It wasn't around for long, as smart was losing loads of cash on every one it built, but there are enough roadsters and roadster-coupés on the used market to keep buyers satisfied.

The on-paper performance figures aren't tremendous, but the behind-the-wheel driving experience genuinely is. The tiny mid-mounted turbocharged engine revs crazily, the paddle-shift auto transmission works well, and the super-taut suspension helps create one of the best handling/roadholding combinations of its era.

If ever a sports car was designed to put a smile on your face, the smart roadster is it. It's great value second-hand too, as well as dirt cheap to run. Don't miss out.

Vauxhall VX220/Opel Speedster

Built by Lotus and based on the Elise, General Motors' most exciting sports car of recent years really got enthusiasts excited when it burst on to

the scene back in 2001. And quite right too. Here we had a car even better looking than the Elise (well, maybe), more powerful than the Elise, and arguably better handling than the Elise – all three of which were real achievements.

The standard 2.2-litre, 147bhp Vauxhall/Opel engine was eventually replaced by a 2.0-litre, 200bhp turbo – a massive output for such a compact, lightweight sports car. No wonder it could touch 243kmh (151mph) flat out, with 100kmh (62mph) passing by in just 4.7 seconds.

The VX220/Speedster finally died in 2005, but now makes a great used buy. Carbon fibre bodywork is hassle-free and the mechanicals very reliable; not bad for such an exciting sports car, eh?

Daihatsu Copen

One of the most diminutive sportsters of the 21st century, the Copen was a major hit in Japan and a fairly popular niche vehicle in Europe – although not everybody raved about its Toy Town looks. Still, the electrically-operated folding metal roof is neat, and the oh-so-eager 659cc turbocharged high-revving power plant is a real gem.

On paper, this doesn't look like a quick car. But squeeze yourself inside the tiny cockpit, make the most of that crazy little engine, enjoy the super-slick gearchange, and you'll find it feels much faster than it really is – especially with the roof lowered into the boot. Handling is tops, as is the sheer fun factor at all speeds.

With typical Daihatsu reliability in its favour, plus a superb manufacturer's warranty if you're buying one that's less than three years old, owning a used Copen makes a lot of sense. As well as being a huge giggle.

Ford StreetKa

Obviously inspired by the standard Ford Ka and based on the same platform, the seriously cute StreetKa enjoyed a short but successful career from 2003 to '05. Is it a genuine sports car? Well, it's a two-seater convertible with a superb chassis and impressive handling, so we reckon it deserves to be included here.

ABOVE You got an airbag on board the VX220/Speedster, but very little else in the way of standard equipment. Well, who needs carpets anyway? *(Vauxhall)*

BELOW The Copen always looked its best with its electrically operated metal roof stowed in the boot. What a little charmer! *(Daihatsu)*

means low running costs, reasonable residuals, and an all-round painless experience. Worth considering.

Porsche 911 Convertible

The 911's history can get complicated – so aside from the classic models of the '70s and '80s, which version should you choose on today's used market? Your final decision will come down to budget, but if you can afford it we'd suggest you take a look at a 1999-on 996-series Convertible. The all-wheel drive Carrera 4 Tiptronic S model cost the best part of £80,000 in the UK back in '99, but will be available for significantly less than that now. Fortunately.

What a machine: 3.4 litres of glorious sounding flat-six power, with an output of 300bhp and performance to match. The 911 Turbo might have been even more powerful, but it was a crazy machine by comparison. The normally-aspirated Carrera 4 remains the most usable, most tempting 996-series Porsche on today's second-hand market. It also happens to be the most risk-free used-supercar purchase currently available.

Suzuki Cappuccino

Although the minuscule Cappuccino was available in the UK and other European markets only from 1993 to '95, it enjoyed a lengthier

ABOVE Inside and out, the StreetKa was heavily based around the standard Ford Ka hatchback. That did nothing to spoil its cheeky, characterful feel, though. (Ford)

Promoted initially by Kylie Minogue, the StreetKa might be a bit too 'girly' for some tastes. But before you dismiss it, you really should take to the wheel; you might just find yourself impressed with its eager (rather than fast) performance, its nifty handling, and its genuine fun appeal. It's also as sensible a used buy as any other Ford, which

career in Japan before production finally ceased in 1997. Just 1,100 cars were sold in Britain, though others have since arrived as personal imports.

So what makes a used Cappuccino worthy of your budget? Primarily its fun appeal. This 657cc three-cylinder sportster might have developed no more than 63bhp, but the way in which it was delivered was genuinely entertaining. It took eight seconds to hit 100kmh (62mph), but it felt a lot faster. The low-down driving position, the snug cockpit, the rev-happy engine, and the sharp handling all combined to make the tiny Suzuki one of the most characterful, most entertaining sports cars of the '90s. Surely another that's destined for future classic status?

ABOVE As the 911 family developed, so the Convertible versions grew steadily more desirable. Shown here is a 3.6-litre derivative from 1994. *(Porsche)*

FAR LEFT Despite the popularity of the StreetKa, Ford decided to pull the plug after just two and a half years in production. *(Ford)*

LEFT Now largely forgotten by all but a small band of enthusiasts, the Suzuki Cappuccino breathed new life into the affordable sports car scene back in the 1990s. *(Suzuki)*

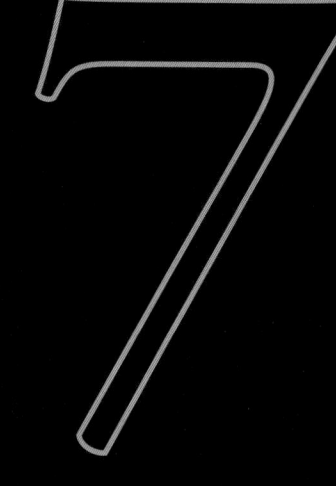

Buying
a used
sports car

**Buying a used sports
car from a dealer is
meant to bring some
reassurance in the UK
thanks to the Sale of
Goods Act.
*(Paul Hardiman)***

Basic precautions

Assuming you've already decided which second-hand sports car best suits your needs – and, just as importantly, which you can afford – it's time to get out there and start checking out a few examples for sale. Before you do that, though, you need to know what you're looking for, what goes wrong, and how you can avoid getting ripped-off.

Before we get on to the specifics of buying a used sports car, however, I'll just offer a few words of caution about buying second-hand cars in general. At the best of times, it's a minefield of dangers and pitfalls; and when you see a sports car that seems to be exactly the one you've been searching high and low for, it's so easy to get carried away in the excitement and forget some basic procedures. And that's when you're particularly vulnerable.

To begin with then, when buying any used vehicle only ever arrange to meet the vendor at their own home or (in the case of a dealer) at their premises. Meeting 'halfway' or arranging to have the car brought to your address is a classic ploy used by vendors who don't actually own the vehicles in question.

When you get to the vendor's house, ask to see the vehicle's V5C Registration Document (assuming you're buying the car in the UK) and check that the vendor's name and the address

OPPOSITE Does the used sports car you're interested in come with a full service history and proof of all work carried out? If not, why not? *(Author)*

LEFT Does that mileage seem genuine? Sports cars are just as likely as any other vehicle to end up being 'clocked', which means you should always be on your guard. *(Author)*

BELOW Has the vehicle ever been the target of thieves or vandals? Look carefully for signs of previous damage when inspecting any sports car. *(Lexus)*

RIGHT If a sports car gets vandalised, it's often its hood that suffers the most damage. Look for signs of abuse. Maybe the hood has recently been replaced? *(MG Rover)*

BELOW When checking over a used sports car, look for mismatched paintwork or uneven panel gaps, both telltale signs of poor post-accident repair work. *(Author)*

shown on the V5C correspond with where you actually are. If you've any doubts or concerns, simply walk away. And if there's no V5C offered with the vehicle at all, don't buy the car under any circumstances, no matter how tempting it seems.

Checking the genuineness of a sportster goes much further, though. Still with the V5C in your hand, take a look at the car's VIN number. Check it against the number that's printed on the V5C, and if there's any discrepancy whatsoever don't even consider buying the vehicle. It's that simple.

At this stage you also need to be looking into the car's service history, to check that what the vendor claims to be a full service history actually is, as well as using this to help verify the mileage. Never accept a vendor's claim that 'the service book is still at the garage; I forgot to pick it up when I had the car serviced last week'. If a service history is boasted about, you want to be able to see it in front of you before you even consider making an offer.

Don't be afraid to spend time carefully studying the service book and any previous MoT certificates that are with the car. Check that all the mileages shown on certain dates seem to tally with what's being claimed about the vehicle. You might even want to make a note of the previous owner's name and address, approaching them before you hand over any money to ensure that they can back-up what you've been told and vouch for the car's history.

Another obvious point when viewing any used sports car is to look for signs of forced entry, which relates to the previous point about checking the vendor's actual ownership. It's a sad fact of life that sports cars are particularly popular with thieves (and many sports cars are annoyingly vulnerable too), so any signs of a previous break-in may simply have occurred during the current keeper's ownership. Don't be afraid to ask, because there's no reason why they should hide this from you. If, however, you can clearly see that a door lock has been forced, the steering column shroud looks strangely loose, the fabric hood looks like it's been damaged in the past, or there are signs of shattered glass inside the car, you've every right to have your suspicions aroused when the vendor denies all knowledge.

Sports cars also tend to be popular targets for vandals, and it's not unusual to see examples with slashed roofs, often damaged just for the sheer hell of it. This is easy for a vendor to hide, simply by having a new convertible hood fitted. However, if the hood hasn't been replaced and there's some obvious damage you should use this as a bargaining tool when buying – as long as you've priced up the cost of a new hood beforehand, of course, as prices do vary hugely from model to model.

You also need to be on the lookout for signs of previous accident damage. Particularly on younger vehicles, check for mismatched paintwork (colour, finish, and so on); ripples in body panels (possible evidence of body filler or poor repair work); signs of 'over-spray'; wheels that seem out of alignment; obvious replacement of 'inner' panel work under the bonnet – the list goes on, but just a couple of these points should be enough to make you suspicious and question the vendor's claim that 'she's never been in an accident'.

How thoroughly you follow this kind of advice will depend partly on how much you're paying for your second-hand sports car, how old it is, and what you're intending to use it for. Let's face it, if a 15-year-old MX-5 is being advertised at what looks like a bargain price and is described in the advert as 'average condition', you can hardly expect it to be the most immaculate example on the street. Be realistic in your approach, as much depends on your own budget and how much work you're willing to carry out once you've bought the car.

One final point worth mentioning before we move on to a few specifics is this: professional car inspections. In the UK, you can pay anything between £100 and £200 or more for an expert to come along and thoroughly examine the vehicle you're thinking of buying. The AA and RAC carry out such inspections, as do many private companies and individuals, and I'd advise anybody thinking of investing in a second-hand sports car to consider having it thoroughly looked at. If the examiner finds any minor faults you might have missed, you'll be able to use this to negotiate the price downwards; and if he discovers something major that makes you think twice about buying the car at all, that's also money well spent.

Such examinations usually include an HPI (or similar) check to ensure the sports car in question has never been registered as stolen,

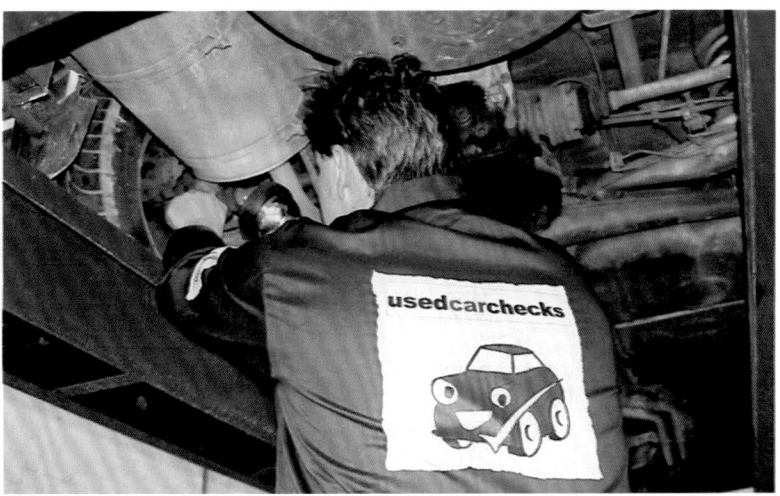

previously written-off in an accident, or still has any outstanding finance against it. This is essential information, and it's available to anybody with a phone and a credit card to pay for it. Even if you decide against a full independent inspection of a used vehicle, failure to have an HPI check carried out can be a very expensive lesson to learn. The difference in value between a 'clean' second-hand sports car and one that's been previously written-off and repaired can be 50 per cent or more, so we're talking serious money here. Before you buy any car of reasonable value in the UK, give HPI a call on 01722 422422 and get all the checks done. If everything is clear, surely that extra peace of mind is worth every penny of the cost?

ABOVE It's often worth investing in a professional car inspection before you hand over your cash. It could result in money saved if major faults are found. *(Used Car Checks)*

BELOW An essential tool for the used car buyer is a full HPI check to confirm it has never been previously written off or still has outstanding finance against it. *(Author)*

Japanese imports

ABOVE An ex-Japanese 'grey' import MX-5 can be easily identified, partly by its differently shaped rear number plate panel and Eunos badging. *(Author)*

Some, but by no means all, of what you've already read in this chapter won't necessarily apply if it's an unofficially imported Japanese sports car you're thinking of buying, one that's found its way over second-hand from its homeland in recent years.

The most popular 'grey' import by far is the Mazda MX-5 (often badged as a Miata or Eunos), although it's possible for just about any sports car to end up in the UK as a used import from Japan. This can even apply to British and European models, with many examples of the old MG RV8 (most of which ended up being exported to Japan when new, back in the early '90s) being brought back to Britain as used vehicles and sold on to enthusiasts.

With any 'grey' import, you obviously need to carry out the same checks for accident damage, signs of abuse, VIN number matching and so on; that's logical enough. But such issues as service history and previous MoTs aren't quite so straightforward.

The main problem is that a lot of Japanese imports don't come with a service history – and those that do are obviously written in Japanese, which makes deciphering them something of a challenge. Still, even a virtually unreadable service history is better than none, since it still might be possible to see roughly when servicing was carried out by studying some of the dates. But it's not always easy.

Similarly, if a used sports car has only been in the UK a matter of months there's no way it can come with any previous MoT certificates to help verify its mileage – so you need to bear this in mind and be extra scrupulous when giving the car the 'once over'.

This means that, when examining it throughout, not only are you looking for signs of neglect, abuse, accident damage and the like, you're also being vigilant about evidence of non-genuine mileage. If a mileage is indicated at 60,000, for example, you should be happy that the engine is reasonably rattle-free, that there's no excessive smoke when revved, that the interior is tidy and not worn, that the shock absorbers don't feel too soft or wallowing when cornering and that the bodywork's general condition is in keeping with a sports car of such mileage. If you have any doubts at all, or the odd alarm bell is ringing in your head, it's time to look elsewhere; there's certainly no shortage of used 'grey' imports usually on sale.

The best way of ensuring you don't get stung when buying any 'grey' import is to make sure the supplying dealer is a member of the British Independent Motor Trade Association (BIMTA), an established organisation that, in the event of a dispute between a member of the public and an importer, can get involved and offer a conciliatory service – but only if the company concerned is a current member.

There's even more usefulness to BIMTA than that, though. When buying from a BIMTA member, make sure you ask them to provide an official Certificate of Authenticity to confirm whether or not a vehicle was ever registered as stolen prior to being exported from Japan, as well as proving there's no outstanding finance on it. BIMTA can also provide odometer checks – and, again, this is a must if you're in any doubt about the imported car you're buying or the dealer you're buying it from. The vast majority of imports are sold in Japan via one of the country's 140 auction houses, and BIMTA has access to the records of

almost all of them. This means an official odometer check can ascertain how many kilometres a vehicle had covered by the time it went under the hammer in Japan, making it easy for any buyer to prove whether or not it has since been 'clocked'.

As long as the 'grey' sports car you're buying is registered in the UK, has passed an ESVA test (if applicable, as this only applies to vehicles under ten years of age), comes with a BIMTA Certificate of Authenticity, and appears to be in decent condition, the risks involved are realistically no greater than when buying a UK-spec model.

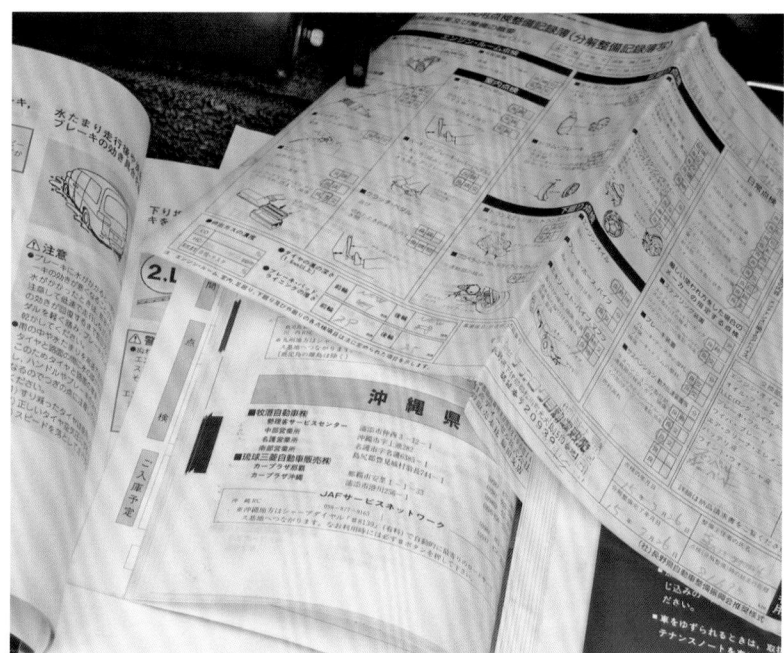

ABOVE Some 'grey' imports come with a full service history, albeit written in Japanese! Still, something's better than nothing … *(Author)*

BELOW Buying a 'grey' import? Checking out its history and genuineness via a BIMTA certificate is money well spent. *(Author)*

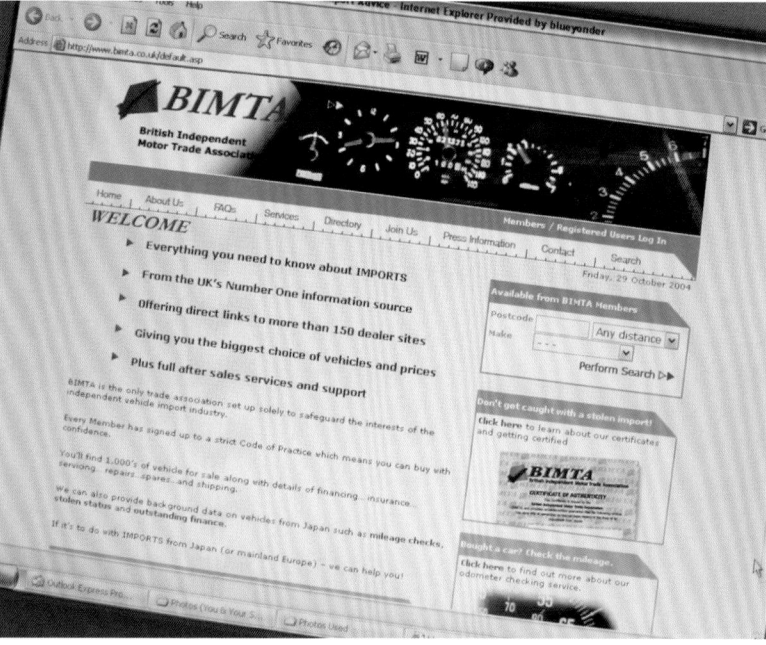

What goes wrong?

Whatever kind of sports car you're thinking of buying, there will inevitably be things that go wrong with it, either through age or mileage. Or both. That's a simple fact of buying any used vehicle, even if it happens to be a Japanese-built sportster with a superb reputation for reliability.

It's important you carry out some of your own research before scouring the classified ads and entering the used car jungle. Check out some of the specific buyers' reports for your make and model (both online and in car magazines) to find out if there are any particular weak spots you should be aware of, as this could save you a considerable sum of money in the future.

For instance, is the sports car you're thinking of buying a turbocharged model? If so, you need to check that the turbo unit itself is fully functioning before you hand over your cash. Excessive smoke from the exhaust can be a sign of turbo wear; and you'll also need to check that as the revs rise in each gear you can feel the turbo spinning into action, resulting in that all-important increase in acceleration as the turbo starts to do its job. If you've any doubts, it may be worth getting a professional turbo inspection carried out before you buy; and if the vendor claims there's been a new turbo fitted in the last year or two, insist on seeing a receipt or guarantee to prove this.

It's important to check the transmission, suspension, and steering of any second-hand sports car you're thinking of buying, as an uncaring owner who has constantly thrashed the car will have accelerated the wear process. Shock absorbers that are badly worn through heavy use or high mileage, as an example, will drastically affect the previously excellent handling characteristics of your car – as well as being expensive to replace in some instances. It certainly pays to be on your guard.

Modern power steering systems tend to be reliable even at high mileages, though it's not unusual to see leaks from the power steering box. While you're under there, check for engine and transmission oil leaks too – not necessarily a major problem depending on your own expectations, but certainly something you should be aware of.

Assuming the car's braking system is fairly standard in design, there should be few things to worry about on a well-maintained example, though you should still be on the lookout for often overlooked problems like warped discs, which can be pricey to replace. Check this whilst you're taking a look at the whole braking circuit for signs of neglect and wear. And if anti-lock brakes and perhaps even traction control are fitted, ensure during your test-drive that these appear to be working as they should.

Auto Express Car Search

News | Previews | Road Tests | New Cars | Used Cars

CLICK HERE TO REVEAL

Enter Search... GO

LVL 00

Welcome: Guest

REGISTER
LOGIN

SECTIONS
PRODUCT TEST
CRASH TEST
PICTURE GALLERY
VIDEO GALLERY
CONTACT US
SUBSCRIBE
SHOWROOM

Used Car Road Tests

Index | Archive

April 2002

Lotus Elise

When the original build-it-yourself Elan was killed off in favour of the plush Elite back in 1974, Lotus lost sight of what it does best – making affordable yet advanced sports cars.

But in 1996 the firm launched the Elise, a modern interpretation of founder Colin Chapman's 7. With many available on the used scene now, is this a chance to own one of the finest driver's cars ever, or will unreliability keep yours stuck on the driveway?

Driving

The Elise means fun, fun, fun. Missing modern niceties such as power-steering and ABS, this Lotus puts the accent on driver work rate. No wonder it's been hailed as the spiritual successor to the original Lotus 7.

Thanks to their lively MGF-sourced engines and lightweight racer type-construction, all can hit 60mph in around six seconds. Yet it's not the Elise's pace that amazes, but its race-

More Images

Lotus Elise Offers

Find a New Lotus Elise at Moneysupermarket

Register & Bid on a Lotus Elise at eBay.co.uk

ABOVE Checking the state of any used sports car's steering, suspension, and brakes is an essential way of avoiding hassle and expense at a later date. *(Jaguar)*

RIGHT Damaged brake discs, worn pads, and leaking cylinders are so easily overlooked when inspecting a used sports car. It pays to be vigilant. *(Author)*

BELOW It's unusual for any MX-5 to suffer major rust. However, it still pays to check its sills, door bottoms, footwells, and boot floor for early signs of corrosion. *(Mazda)*

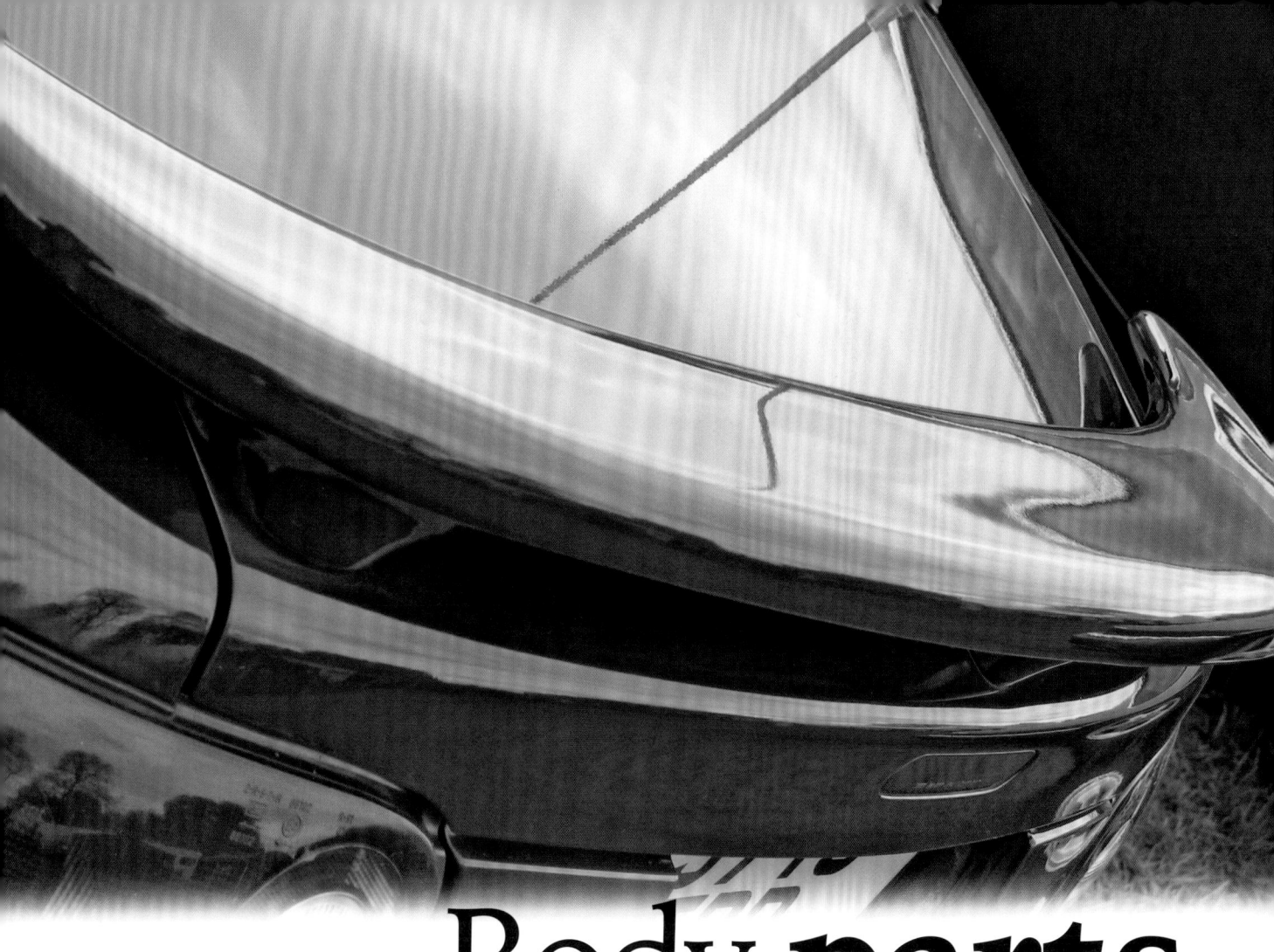

Body parts

An important part of buying any used sports car is to pay careful attention to its bodywork and underside, although your priorities will vary according to the age and price of the vehicle in question. As mentioned earlier, it's unfair to expect a cheap and cheerful old sports car to be cosmetically pristine, but if it comes with a current MoT and is claimed to be in usable condition, then it should at least be structurally sound and capable of regular, safe use.

No matter how reliable a sports car may be by reputation, it's important to remember that any neglected example will eventually rust. It's a fact of life. Many sports cars of the 1990s onwards have made use of galvanised steel, which obviously reduces the risks massively. But if such a car has previously been involved in an accident and has had poor quality panel repairs carried out (or perhaps non-genuine new panels fitted), you could still see signs of creeping corrosion setting in. Don't just assume that all is well.

Even a sports car with an excellent reputation for bodywork longevity will eventually start to deteriorate, and it's possible now to see early Series I Mazda MX-5s with rust around their sills, to their floor pans, and in the boot. Well-maintained examples are usually still in excellent condition, but you should carry out careful checks before you hand over your money. Fail to spot any early signs of corrosion or some rust-disguising

ABOVE Check all outer panels on any steel-bodied sportster for signs of bubbling paintwork and creeping rust. Are there signs of previous repair work, perhaps? *(Author)*

body filler and you could end up spending a lot on future repair work.

Before you start inspecting any used sports car's bodywork, though, don't forget to get clear in your mind what's really important to you. If you don't mind the odd bit of cosmetic corrosion on a wheel arch or along the bottom of a door because you're a realist and you know you're not paying a lot for the vehicle anyway, that's fine – assuming, of course, that the vehicle is still structurally sound and safe. But if you're paying more and you expect your used sportster to be not just solid but impressively smart too, then read on.

Every sports car has its own particular weak areas when it comes to bodywork and corrosion, though the same basic rules apply in most cases. Pay particular attention, for example, to front wings (particularly around light units and the extremities of the wheelarches), the rear arches, the boot lid, the bonnet edges, the bottoms of both doors, and the sills. And beware of any plastic sill or

wheelarch extensions that are fitted, as these can hide serious rust chomping away behind them. Don't assume that a bit of bubbling paintwork is just that; it's invariably a sign of something far more sinister, and will be the result of rust working its way inside-out.

Rust can also break out around the base of the windscreen, near the bulkhead, a difficult job to have repaired properly on any vehicle. In any case, if the car you're looking at is so rusty round its screen that it needs welding repairs, you have to ask yourself whether the inevitably dubious state of the rest of the vehicle makes the task worthwhile.

It's not unusual to find a rotten floor on any elderly sports car, with previous leaks and hard use inevitably taking their toll. Damp and water inside a sports car can lead to rusty foot wells, while a host of mud traps under some models is enough to start encouraging the rusting process from beneath.

BELOW An elderly sports car with a leaking hood has often endured a lifetime of damp carpets, which will inevitably lead to a corroded floorpan in time. Check very carefully. *(Andrew Noakes)*

Other **materials**

Of course, not every sports car is of conventional monocoque steel construction. Some of the more specialist models are built using different materials – which means different things to look out for when viewing.

If you buy a second-hand Lotus Elise, for example, you'll find a chassis made of epoxy-bonded aluminium extrusions and a composite bodyshell. If you choose an ageing Reliant Scimitar SS1 or SST you'll have a separate galvanised steel chassis mounted with glassfibre bodywork. And if you decide on an oh-so-traditional Morgan 4/4 or Plus 8 as your used sports car of choice, you'll find it's of ash-framed construction with body panels made largely of hand-rolled aluminium. The world of specialist sports cars is complex and varied!

The simple solution to all this is, as ever, to make sure you do some research before even considering viewing any cars. Decide on a particular make and model that you're interested in, find out all you can about the way it's constructed, and then talk to other owners, club members, and specialist dealers (as well as grabbing as much information as you can from the Internet) about what exactly is involved.

If, for example, it's a glassfibre-bodied sports car that you're most tempted by, are there particular areas that are prone to cracking or crazing? Are there any notorious trouble spots, such as weak door hinges that cause the doors to drop? If the bodywork was originally self-coloured rather than sprayed after construction, how easy is it to have minor repair work carried out? The more questions like this you can answer about the model that tempts you, the more prepared you'll be when the time comes to go viewing cars. And that means a drastically reduced chance of getting ripped off.

ABOVE Aluminium panels built around an ash frame mark the more traditional Morgans out as a real blast from the past. *(Morgan)*

ABOVE Every Reliant sports car ever built has made use of a steel chassis and glassfibre bodyshell, the soft-top Scimitar GTC being no exception. *(Reliant)*

RIGHT Major glassfibre damage like this is easy to spot. Also be on the lookout, though, for minor crazing and cracks, as well as drooping doors. *(Author)*

ROADSTER EUNOS				
1994 MAZDA MX-5 GREEN
Unusual standard UK model 1.8 engine	14	£1,750.00	3h 42m	United Ki...
1991 MAZDA MX-5 GREEN 1.6 LTD EDITION MX5	4	£1,750.00	4h 11m	United K...
1991 MAZDA MX-5 SILVER, taxed and tested	13	£1,220.00	4h 32m	United K...
1990 MAZDA MX-5 RED	2	£1,070.00	5h 36m	United ...
MAZDA MX-5 1.6 MONACO
NO RESERVE	-	£3,000.00	7h 13m	United ...
1995 MAZDA MX-5 BLUE		£4,750.00	20h 10m	United...

Where to find them

Narrowing down your choice of second-hand car isn't the only major decision to be made here. You also need to consider whether you'll be buying privately, from a trader, or even via a car auction.

Buying your used sportster from a dealer certainly brings the greatest consumer rights in the UK, with more comeback available to you if things go wrong. Buying from a dealer means you're covered by the Sale of Goods Act, which essentially means the car you're spending your hard-earned cash on must meet an acceptable standard. It's also a relatively simple way of buying, as you can peruse several vehicles on one dealer's forecourt without the need to travel great distances to view privately advertised examples.

As ever, though, there are pitfalls to be aware of. First of all, you need to ensure the dealer you're talking to is a member of a trade association, such as the Retail Motor Industry Federation in the UK –

ABOVE The principle of using an online auction is similar to a traditional auction house: if you're the winning bidder, you're legally obliged to complete the sale. *(Author)*

ABOVE Most auction houses are full of mainstream models, though sometimes something sporty, interesting, and rather tempting passes through …
(British Car Auctions)

OPPOSITE Decided on a particular make and model? Visiting your nearest franchised dealer could bring the biggest choice of second-hand examples, without the hassle of travelling long distances.
(Author)

or, if it's a company specialising in 'grey' imports, BIMTA (mentioned earlier in the chapter). Secondly, you need to ensure you understand exactly the terms under which the vehicle is being sold to you. For example, is the dealer claiming some kind of warranty is included in the sale, and if so, has he given you an opportunity to study the small print, the various exclusions, and the timescale? Some dealers offer their own 30-day all-inclusive warranty, while others will try to sell you a one-, two-, or even three-year independent used car warranty – on which they will obviously be earning commission. Use a warranty as a useful haggling tool, but make sure you understand exactly what is and isn't part of its coverage.

You also need to be realistic about the age of the sports car you're buying from a dealer, as your consumer rights are very much affected by this. You have every legal right to expect a twelve-month-old sports car purchased from a dealer to be in superb condition throughout, unless he stipulates otherwise. But a ten- or fifteen-year-old example will inevitably have experienced wear and tear – which means that if the exhaust fails, the brake pads need replacing, or the battery dies

after a few days of ownership, you'll have very little cause for complaint. It's an old vehicle and, quite simply, parts do wear out. It's a fact of life.

Before buying any used sports car from a dealer, you should also check the terms of the sale itself, as elderly vehicles are often marked on invoices as 'Trade Sales'. This is even firmer proof that you're buying the vehicle 'as seen', you're happy to take the risk, and there are no guarantees as to its condition. It can be a good way of grabbing a bargain, but not if you're a cautious buyer who doesn't enjoy taking the odd risk.

Buying privately can be a risky business too, although it can also save you money. The only real legal obligation of a private seller is that the vehicle must be sold 'as described' – and that's about it. The seller isn't obliged to offer any kind of guarantees, you won't get a warranty, and it's unlikely you'll be able to part-exchange your old car. On the other hand, a private seller doesn't have the overheads of a trader, which means you can often get a used sports car cheaper this way.

The most effective way of taking the risk out of buying privately is to ensure you get an HPI check carried out, as detailed earlier on in this chapter. And, as already mentioned, it's worth considering a professional car inspection by an independent expert. It could save you a considerable sum in the long run.

The third major source of used sports cars, of course, is an auction house, although most general car auctions only feature a small percentage of 'interesting' cars among their more mainstream stock. Car auctions in general bring their own set of rules and consumer rights, of which you should be aware before you attend. For a start, there's usually no opportunity to test-drive any vehicles being sold at auction, as the sales process happens so quickly. Also, those auction houses offering any cars with what they call a trial will be giving some kind of guarantee on the condition of the engine and transmission only, with absolutely nothing else included. Most older vehicles are sold 'as seen', which means no comeback whatsoever.

When buying at auction, bear in mind that a buyer's premium will be charged on top of your winning bid, so you need to find out how much this is in advance. And, of course, don't forget that your winning bid is legally binding and means you have entered into a contract with the auctioneers from which you are then unable to withdraw.

What many people don't realise is that similar rules and regulations apply to Internet auction sites, so don't be tempted to enter a bid on any sports car listed on eBay 'as a bit of a laugh' unless you're serious about buying it. If you win the online auction and don't proceed with the purchase for any reason, the vendor has every right to take legal proceedings against you.

So are auctions a good idea? Well, they can certainly yield some bargains. But they're not for the fainthearted, and buyers should take every precaution before placing a bid. Get it right, though – ideally taking somebody with you to help check the vehicles you're interested in – and you can end up with a trade-price sportster that's exactly what you've been looking for. It does happen.

One final word of warning about online auctions in particular, though – and that's to make sure your common sense doesn't desert you when browsing the Internet. Is it really worth bidding several thousand pounds on a sports car you've never even seen, let alone driven? There's a good chance that the seller is honest and genuine, but do you really want to take that risk? Go and see the car for yourself before the auction ends unless you're happy to end up seriously out of pocket. Tempting photographs alone don't make a used sports car a good buy.

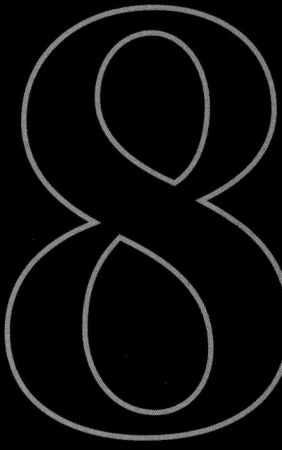

Classic collection

Today's classic sports
car scene is thriving,
with new enthusiasts
tempted by the many
and varied models on
offer. *(LAT)*

Decisions, decisions ...

The biggest dilemma, of course, is narrowing down your choice of classic sportsters – a task that's often even more difficult than it sounds when you start looking at your own priorities and the numbers of potential models that seem to fit the bill perfectly.

These days, a sports car doesn't even need to be a certain age in order to be universally viewed as a classic, a point we take a more in-depth look at in the next chapter. That's why models like the Series I Mazda MX-5, for example, are now seen by most as classics, even though sales in the UK and many other export markets didn't get under way until as relatively recently as 1990. In classic car terms, that's a modern vehicle; but the MX-5's fantastic design and its legendary role as re-creator of the classic sports car concept both combine to ensure its classic status in the twenty-first century.

So, if relatively modern sports cars like the MX-5, the front-wheel-drive Lotus Elan, and even the MGF are now looked upon as modern classics rather than merely second-hand, where does that leave the more traditional end of the classic car scene? Doing pretty well for itself, is the obvious answer. You see, for every enthusiast who will defend the classic status of the Mazda MX-5, there will be plenty more doing the same for older, undisputed classics like the MGA of the 1950s, the Alfa Romeo Duetto Spider of the 1960s, and the Triumph Stag of the 1970s. These are the sports cars that are now looked upon with nostalgic fondness, the kind of sports cars you'll see on a regular basis in classic car magazines the world over, and at classic car shows everywhere throughout the summer months.

So before you start narrowing down your list of classic sports cars worth considering, you should perhaps ask yourself whether you lust after a sportster of the '60s or prefer the obvious advantages of a more modern classic. For many enthusiasts, it's a tough call. The older classics often tend to be the most characterful, as anybody who has ever piloted an Austin-Healey 'Frogeye' Sprite, an MGA, or – further up the price scale – a Jaguar E-Type will testify. By definition, though, they also tend to come with the most potential problems, partly because they weren't all designed for high-mileage motoring (unlike more recent cars) and partly because they've had longer for serious rust problems to set in. An early MX-5 or MGF will be more reliable in daily use, less rust-prone, and more suited to long journeys, but much of the charm and charisma that many classic car traditionalists look for in a sportster will be missing. And this is why it's important to be honest with yourself about your own priorities.

Another point to bear in mind about more modern classics is that they haven't necessarily stopped depreciating yet. Buy yourself a decent classic sports car from the 1950s, '60s. or '70s and, as long as you maintain it well and look after it properly, it should maintain its value during your period of ownership. But if you opt for a mid-1990s Mazda MX-5 instead, you'll find its value hasn't necessarily 'bottomed-out' yet – which means there's still some depreciation to come.

In Chapter Nine we take a look at the various running costs involved in buying a classic sports car. But even before you start looking, you should be aware of some of the most fundamental differences – and how they might affect you and your bank balance.

OPPOSITE What makes a classic? Despite the relative modernity of the first-generation MX-5, most enthusiasts reckon it's already worthy of classic status. *(Mazda)*

LEFT While modern classics are rapidly gaining in popularity, more traditional classic offerings like the Triumph Stag continue to attract dedicated enthusiasts. *(British Leyland)*

BELOW Investing in an undisputed classic like an MG Midget means depreciation should be a thing of the past – as long as you maintain the car well and keep it in tip-top condition. *(Author)*

Older, wiser?

ABOVE Modified since its pre-war days, MG's T-series was updated into TF guise in 1953, providing a couple more years of success before the arrival of the all-new MGA in '55. (MG Rover)

Between World Wars 1 and 2, the popularity of the sports car grew immensely, with some seriously successful models from companies like Bentley, MG, and Morgan grabbing the limelight in various sectors of the market. But it was after World War 2 and on into the 1950s that the sports car concept gathered pace and moved more into the mainstream.

Being prepared to consider a classic sports car from the 1950s brings a fascinating array of models to your potential shopping list, with one of the most famous sporting marques of all time – MG – providing much of the interest.

Up until 1955, MG relied upon a heavily revised version of the pre-war T-series design to carry it through, with the '53-on TF being a successful update of an ageing model range. Although still unmistakably pre-war in its aesthetics, the adoption of a lower bonnet line and sloping front grille gave the TF a more modern stance than the TD that preceded it. And with such improvements as a more powerful 1.5-litre engine (from 1954), rack and pinion steering, and coil-sprung independent front suspension, the TF was also a far better car to drive than MG's proper pre-war offerings.

Even so, the launch of the MGA in 1955 didn't come a moment too soon. In fact, it's difficult to imagine more of a contrast to the TF's ancient looks than the MGA's all-new sleek, modern, handsome styling. With BMC's 1,489cc B-series engine providing the power, and independent front suspension and rack and pinion steering adding to the driving enjoyment, the all-new A was a marvel – and one that only got better as the years wore on. The limited-production MGA Twin Cam arrived in 1958, though the following year saw the most important update of all in the shape of the new MGA 1600. With 80–86bhp on tap, plus front disc brakes and a host of other useful improvements, the 1600 was the best of the 'normal' MGAs and remains a sought-after machine to this day. As 1950s sports cars go, it's surely one of the best all-rounders.

While all this was going on with MG, specialist manufacturer Morgan was busy replacing its ancient three-wheeler line-up with a range of new four-wheeled sportsters, the first example for the 1950s being the 4/4 Series II of 1955 onwards. Despite offering just 36bhp from its 1,172cc sidevalve Ford engine, the latest 4/4 was a likeable machine, its biggest hindrance being the rather grim three-speed gearbox. Less than 400 examples were produced in total, and nowadays it's a rare sight.

Rather more upmarket than this throughout the 1950s was the awesomely desirable Jaguar XK range, the first of which – the XK120 – actually

arrived as early as 1948. The range continued to be developed throughout the '50s, before finally being replaced by the even more stunning E-Type in 1961. These days, of course, any Jaguar XK fetches serious money; but, if you can afford one, you'll find it a joy to own and one of the most effective ways of generating envy at any classic car event.

Deciding which Jaguar XK makes the most desirable choice largely comes down to personal preference, though for our money an XK140 Roadster or Drophead-Coupé would take some beating. Easily the most handsome of the range in the author's opinion, the XK140 of 1954–7 offered

ABOVE While MG was modernising its line-up, Morgan stayed with its traditional 4/4 model, available with sidevalve power and a choice of two or four seats. *(Morgan)*

BELOW The vital new MGA took the Abingdon marque in a fresh, modern direction for the second half of the 1950s – and not before time. *(MG Rover)*

ABOVE Any Jaguar XK
Roadster or Drophead-
Coupé is a seriously
desirable – and rather
expensive – classic
choice these days. One
of the highlights of the
1950s, surely? *(Author)*

RIGHT Triumph's
TR range enjoyed
great success in the
'50s, with the TR3A
being a particularly
popular sporting choice
among enthusiasts.
(John Colley)

modern updates like rack and pinion steering combined with a standard power output of 190bhp – seriously big news back then. Inevitably, though, any XK140 in excellent condition will mean a hefty outlay for an interested purchaser nowadays.

Usefully more affordable than an XK are the MGA-rivalling Triumph TR2, TR3, and TR3A models of 1953–61, a range of two-seater open-top sports cars with 1,991cc four-cylinder power, offering up to 100bhp on later versions. All three models are closely related, sharing basically similar curvaceous styling and distinctive cutaway-doors design.

By far the most successful of the early TRs was the TR3A of 1957 onwards, with more than 58,000 produced in total, of which a large proportion went for export. There are survivors around that have been well restored over the years, and it's certainly worth tracking down the very best you can afford. But many enthusiasts prefer the later TR4–TR6 models and their superior performance and sportier feel. If that's you, we'll take a look at them a little further on.

For the ultimate charm from a 1950s sports car, though, you need look no further than one of the most diminutive, most basic models of the time: the utterly lovable first-generation Austin-Healey 'Frogeye' Sprite. It ran for just three years (1958–61), paving the way for the subsequent Sprites and MG Midgets of the '60s, yet the 'Frogeye' will always be remembered for its character and charisma. Power came from the 948cc version of BMC's A-series engine, which meant the 'Frogeye' was eager rather than fast. But that didn't matter; this little gem is still regarded as one of the most fun-to-drive classics of its era.

There was no shortage of specialist British firms producing desirable (or certainly interesting) sports cars during the 1950s, of course, with the likes of Aston Martin, Lotus, Turner, AC, Berkeley, and Healey achieving varying levels of success. And in Continental Europe, too, the sports car scene was taking off, with models like the Alfa Romeo Giulietta Spider, Porsche 356A Speedster, and Mercedes-Benz 190SL and 300SL Roadsters all appearing during the 1950s. But it was in the '60s that the sports car market really hit the big time – and that's the era many enthusiasts choose when it comes to buying a classic sports car today.

ABOVE One of the most lovable, most characterful sports cars of all time? What the 'Frogeye' Sprite lacks in power it more than makes up for in charisma. *(Author)*

Choosing a '60s sportster

It's the decade that so many people relate to in terms of music, fashion, and cars, and it's still one of the most popular eras when it comes to classic sports cars. So which 1960s models are the most worthy of consideration now, four decades on?

If you fancy a diminutive sportster that's nippy, economical, and enormous fun to drive, you can't get much better than the 1961-on MG Midget or its re-badged cousin, the Austin-Healey Sprite Mk II. Both models saw various improvements during the '60s, though their character and fun appeal remained intact throughout. Engine size increased from 948cc to 1,098cc, ending up at 1,275cc by 1966. The Midget is a far easier car to track down than the Sprite, due to its greater sales figures, but either model will provide plenty of smiles per mile, as well as impressively low running costs.

If a Midget doesn't appeal, its 1960s archrival, the Triumph Spitfire, might. Launched in '62, the

first of the Spitfires is now quite a rare little beast but well worth seeking out. Most usable Spitfire of the '60s, though, is the Series III model that ran from 1967 to 1970, offering 1,296cc power (in place of the previous 1,147cc unit), better performance, and a raised bumper height to create a new front-end look. Rust is the biggest enemy of any Triumph Spitfire, but well maintained or carefully restored examples are out there, and they can still be picked up without spending a fortune.

Even smaller than the Midget and the Spitfire were Japan's most adventurous sporting offerings of the late '60s, the Honda S500 and S800. These miniature marvels were years ahead of their

ABOVE The Spitfire was developed throughout the 1960s and beyond, enjoying several power hikes and this very successful restyle along the way. *(Triumph)*

OPPOSITE From 1961, buyers of affordable sports cars had a choice of Austin-Healey Sprite Mk II (shown here) or MG Midget – each virtually identical in all but name. *(British Motor Corporation)*

LEFT Japan was keen to grab a slice of the sports car action, hence the arrival of the miniature Honda S500 and S800 models. *(Author)*

ABOVE The launch of the Elan was a big step forward for Lotus. This was the company's most sophisticated little sportster to date, and enjoyed instant success. *(LAT)*

RIGHT Replacing the MGA in 1962, the new MGB was bigger, more powerful, and more in tune with '60s-style tastes. It went on to become one of the longest-running MG models of all time. *(Author)*

time, with the S800 boasting a quad-carb 791cc twin-cam engine, front disc brakes, and independent front suspension. It was never a mass-seller in Europe (it was never intended to be), but as one of the most fascinating little sports cars to appear during the 1960s, the S800 was unrivalled in its class. Available in hard-top coupé or soft-top convertible guise, this gem of a Japanese sportster now boasts a small but extremely loyal following.

Inevitably, however, such cars are simply too small or too underpowered for many potential buyers tempted by the products of the '60s – which is where models like the MGB, Triumph TR4/TR4A/TR5/TR6, Alfa Romeo Spider, Sunbeam Alpine/Tiger, and Lotus Elan come into their own. And what a tempting line-up they make for any prospective classic sports car buyer.

Most 'specialist' of that little lot is inevitably the Lotus Elan, the car that brought the Norfolk company instant fame for the quality of its handling and its eager performance when it debuted in 1962. Arguably at its best in S1 to S4 guises (though the 126bhp Sprint of 1970–3 has to be the ultimate if money is no object), the original Elan combined cute, characterful styling with one of the ultimate sports car driving experiences of the 1960s. And with glassfibre bodywork there was obviously no outer-panel rust to worry about; on the other hand, the backbone chassis would corrode and the glassfibre itself could crack and craze with the passing of time…

Corrosion is something often associated (sometimes unfairly) with Italian classics, but that doesn't mean the original Alfa Romeo Duetto Spider isn't a sensational choice. The Spider's styling was spoiled slightly by 1970 thanks to a cut-off rear end rather than the gently sloping version of the original; but really, any Alfa Spider from the model's early years has a charismatic, fun, and seriously engaging sports car driving style.

Britain's sports car industry was at its most successful in the 1960s, with the '62-on MGB proving the best-seller for many years. In soft-top Roadster guise, the B was always available solely with 1,798cc B-series power (used elsewhere in the BMC line-up), although 1967–9 saw a total of 4,542 MGC Roadsters being produced – essentially an MGB fitted with an ex-Austin-Healey 2,912cc straight-six engine.

The MGB remains one of today's most popular classic choices, combining decent styling with simple mechanicals, easy maintenance, superb parts availability, and a pleasant driving style. It might not be the fastest or best-handling classic

sportster for your money, but it's one of the most sensible, most practical options available.

For some, of course, an MGB is just too predictable a choice – so why not consider a Triumph TR instead? From the 1960s you have a choice of TR4 (1961–4), TR4A (1964–7), TR5/TR250 (1967–8), and TR6 (1968–75), offering 1,991cc or 2,138cc four-cylinder power in most cases – apart from the brutish TR6, whose 2,498cc straight-six power plant boasted up to 150bhp and sounded glorious. Whichever 1960s TR you choose, you'll revel in its oh-so-British feel and its classic appeal. And with the back-up of a thriving Triumph club scene and a good choice of marque specialists offering spares and restoration services, you'll soon feel part of an enthusiastic community. Buy the best original example you can afford (or, if it's previously been restored, satisfy yourself that it's been done to a high standard) and

ABOVE From the Rootes Group came the Sunbeam Alpine and Tiger models, a couple of similar looking sportsters with dramatically different personalities and power sources. *(Author)*

BELOW Not as pretty as the earliest Duetto models, any classic Alfa Romeo Spider now makes a tempting buy for anybody who fancies an Italian twist to their sports car motoring. *(Alfa Romeo)*

ABOVE The popularity of the E-type as the world's sexiest, most beautiful sports car shows no signs of abating, thanks in no small part to enthusiasts like Philip Porter, a specialist writer on all things Jaguar. *(Jaguar)*

enjoy being a part of one of the most successful, most satisfying sports car line-ups of all time.

But if MGs and Triumphs really aren't for you, it's worth considering the Rootes Group's sporting offerings of the '60s: the Sunbeam Alpine and Tiger. With neat, period-looking styling and the classic two-seater soft-top layout, these seemed like fairly predictable choices at first glance; and, indeed, the Alpine was pretty conventional, powered as it was by 1,592cc and 1,725cc engines that had given solid service in the Hillman Minx of the time. But the Tiger was something else, boasting (in Series II guise) a 4,727cc ex-Mustang V8 engine capable of churning out up to 200bhp. That was sensational news back in the late '60s, catapulting the now rare Tiger to instant fame. But if that's just a bit too much for you, any well preserved Alpine nowadays makes a likeable, practical, and fun-to-drive classic sportster.

Not every sports car of the 1960s, of course, was for the everyman, some of the most memorable and iconic designs being positively upmarket. The Austin-Healey 3000 of 1959–68, for example, was a stylish all-Brit offering that did rather well for itself in the USA. And with up to 150bhp available in its final Mk III guise, this was a terrific roadster for any enthusiast driver when it came to behind-the-wheel thrills.

But surely the ultimate sports car of the decade has to be the legendary Jaguar E-Type, the 1961 sensation that, in Roadster guise, continued right through to '74, and proved to be the Coventry marque's most admired creation of all time. With 3.8- and 4.2-litre straight-six power plants – or the awesome 5.3-litre V12 for the 1971-on Series III models – the E-Type proved itself a formidable high-performance machine, with even the earliest, smallest-engined Series I offering well over 140mph flat out.

The world had never before seen a production sports car quite like the E-Type, its monstrously long bonnet, sleek profile, fantastic aerodynamics and supercar-like performance putting the newcomer well and truly in a class of its own. And it's a machine that's as adored and revered today as it's ever been.

These days, you can go out and spend the price of an entry-level BMW 5-Series on a superb Jaguar E-Type if you want to – but would that be a sensible move? Certainly not for everyday use, as any relatively complex classic car is going to suffer (both bodily and mechanically) if forced to endure twenty-first-century motoring on a daily basis. But can you think of a sexier, more desirable, summer-use classic to have parked in your garage than a stunning E-Type? Even almost half a century on from its debut, this is still a classic sportster without compare.

The '70s options

If the idea of a sports car from the 1970s appeals more than a '60s offering, what will you be getting for your money? Well, pretty much the same, is the obvious answer, albeit with the odd minor twist. And that's because such classics of the '60s as the MGB and Midget, Triumph Spitfire and TR6, and the Alfa Romeo Spider continued well into (and in some cases well beyond) the new decade.

Admittedly, modifications did arrive. The Midget and B were treated to controversial black 'rubber' bumpers in 1975 to meet new American safety legislation; the Spitfire was upgraded to 1.5-litre power to create the logically-named Spitfire 1500; and the Spider went through a whole series of gradual upgrades and power hikes to keep its competitive edge. But in essence these machines were pretty much as they had been during the previous decade.

Don't make the mistake, though, of assuming every sports car of the 1970s was a warmed-over version of an ageing design. The sports car scene may have been under intense pressure due to worldwide recession and ever more stringent legislation, but that didn't stop some genuinely exciting new designs from arriving. And the first of those burst on to the scene in '69, ready for the new 1970 model year: the Triumph Stag.

Created by Italian styling house Michelotti, the Stag was a handsome, V8-powered grand tourer

ABOVE Most controversial changes to the MGB occurred in the mid-1970s, when a raised ride height and new-look black bumpers inflicted an appearance that horrified the company's more traditional customers. *(Author)*

ABOVE The MG Midget suffered equally to the B at the hands of the stylists in 1975, with the obligatory black 'rubber' bumpers giving it a clumsy look. *(British Leyland)*

with a revolutionary targa-type roll-bar (albeit with a conventional soft-top hood) and an effortless driving style that suited its upmarket status just perfectly. Its brand new engine offered 145bhp and a fantastic soundtrack to match; sadly, though, it was this engine that would eventually prove to be the Stag's downfall.

The Stag received rave reviews upon its launch, and was soon selling well – particularly in the UK and American markets. But it didn't take too long for overheating and head gasket problems to rear their ugly heads, giving the Stag an unenviable reputation for fragility. It limped on for a total of seven years, during which time almost

RIGHT Triumph's Spitfire evolved into Mk IV guise before being treated to a bigger engine for its final Spitfire 1500 incarnation. *(British Leyland)*

26,000 were sold, but an alarming lack of investment from British Leyland meant that the Stag never achieved its full potential and finally faded from the price lists almost unnoticed.

And now? The Triumph Stag is revered as one of the ultimate British classics of all time, with a near fanatical following, terrific club support, and excellent spares availability. Buy a superbly restored example that's had any cooling problems already sorted and you'll find it a joy to own. Just keep up the regular maintenance, won't you?

Rather cheaper than the Stag when new but far more revolutionary by 1970s standards was Italy's Fiat X1/9 – another sportster that endured its fair share of problems but went on to be viewed universally as an icon. This time the problem wasn't fragile mechanicals but a penchant for rusting, its bodywork being prone to major corrosion at an early age. Still, that didn't stop the mid-engined, targa-topped X1/9 from being a major hit, staying in production from 1972 to 1989.

Early X1/9s were powered by Fiat's eager, high-revving 1,290cc four-cylinder engine, though this was soon usurped by the 1,498cc unit fitted to most examples. Meanwhile, its superb weight distribution (thanks to that mid-engined layout) resulted in fantastic handling and roadholding by 1970s standards, allowing any enthusiastic driver to really make the most of what performance there

was. This was a car guaranteed to put a smile on any petrolhead's face.

Also from Italy in the 1970s came the Lancia Beta Spider (a targa-topped version of the Beta Coupé) and the Fiat 124 Spider (built by Pininfarina and the longest-running member of the successful 124 family), both of which stayed in production right through to the '80s. Fun? Of course (I mean, they're Italian). Fragile? Only when it comes to the age-old problem of rust.

So can any of the models from that Italian threesome make sound buys now? Yes, as long as the X1/9, Beta, or 124 you're tempted by is in excellent condition bodily, with no major signs of rust or dodgy repairs. And the same applies to another classic of the '70s, the oft-overlooked Jensen-Healey, a British-built specialist offering that sold almost 11,000 examples between 1972 and '76. With premature rusting and a potentially unreliable ex-Lotus 2.0-litre engine both against it, the Jensen-Healey suffered at the hands of critics. But again, if you find a good one you'll have a worthwhile and genuinely different classic to brag to your friends about.

We couldn't leave the '70s without mentioning one of the most talked about British Leyland offerings of the era: the controversial Triumph TR7. Launched to replace the TR6 in 1975, this wedge-shaped newcomer was like nothing else offered by the company back then. The fact that for the first

BELOW Thinking of buying a classic Fiat X1/9? Great idea. But only buy the best, most rust-free example you can find, won't you? *(Author)*

ABOVE These days,
any well-restored
Jensen-Healey makes
an interesting
alternative to the
inevitable rows of
MGBs at classic car
shows throughout
the UK. (Author)

four years of its life it was also only available in
hard-top coupé guise was certainly a slap in the
face for convertible fans everywhere. Finally,
though, in 1979 the TR7 Convertible was
launched, only to disappear again two years later
when the TR7 line-up was laid to rest.

Poor quality control, a lacklustre engine, grim
reliability, and rust-prone bodywork deterred many
potential TR7 buyers at the time; but that needn't
be the case now. Many survivors have either been
lovingly cared for or extremely well restored, so

only buy the very best example you can afford.
Then you'll enjoy the car's oh-so-1970s charm
and its surprisingly competent driving style without
too many worries. Honestly, a well-sorted TR7 is
worth a second look.

But does a '70s sportster make sense
generally, whichever model you find yourself
attracted to? Usually, yes. But if you crave the
ultimate in hassle-free classic motoring,
something a tad more modern might be the
direction to go in.

RIGHT Fans of proper
sports cars were
disappointed back in
the mid-1970s when
the new Triumph TR7
appeared solely in
coupé guise, with no
soft-top option at all.
(British Leyland)

The **modern** classics

Now we're in the territory of genuine classic sports cars from the 1980s and '90s, of which there are certainly plenty. The following chapter deals with the issue of what makes a sports car a classic (an area that's particularly subjective when talking about fairly recent models), so I won't pre-empt that here.

Suffice to say, though, that if you want classic motoring with a traditional feel but without some of the compromises of a '60s-style car, this is where you need to be looking.

Despite the start of the '80s seeing the demise of such successes as the MGB, Midget, Triumph Spitfire and TR7, in some ways the decade is remembered for ageing models that simply refused to die (the Alfa Spider springs to mind) or top-chopped versions of existing coupés (Jaguar XJ-S anyone?). That doesn't mean, however, that genuinely new and worthwhile sports cars didn't appear. They just tended to be from the smallest, most specialised manufacturers.

The early '80s saw a whole line-up of new, wedge-shaped, razor-sharp models from TVR, all derived from the 1980-on Tasmin Coupé. In convertible guise, these exciting newcomers were always at their best, particularly when (in the case of the 350i, 390i, 400, 420, and 450 models) they came with ex-Rover V8 power. That meant up to a

ABOVE Looking for something less predictable than an MX-5? The Lotus Elan that arrived at the tail end of the '80s could be the perfect answer. *(Author)*

RIGHT The much-loved classic Alfa Romeo Spider enjoyed a particularly long life, the final versions not rolling off the production line until the early 1990s. *(Author)*

massive 319bhp, with performance to match – an astonishing figure for a 1980s compact sports car. Pick a superb, low mileage survivor now and you'll still enjoy thrills-a-plenty.

Rather less exciting but still significant was the Reliant Scimitar SS1 launched in 1986 – a two-seater sportster with rather odd wedge styling and

a choice of dreary four-cylinder Ford power or an ex-Nissan 1.8-litre turbo. The latter went particularly well and was huge fun to drive (although very unpredictable in the wrong hands), but the Scimitar's strange looks and mediocre build quality limited its success. Even the launch of the completely restyled SST version in 1989 did

RIGHT Not a popular choice in its day, the Reliant Scimitar SST is now a fairly rare sight, but makes an interesting classic buy for those with a taste for the unusual. *(Reliant)*

nothing for its popularity, and the model quietly faded away in the early '90s. And now? Any Scimitar of this era makes a cheap and cheerful modern classic, particularly if you have a taste for the unusual.

It wasn't until the end of the '80s that the sports car market really picked up with the launch of the front-wheel-drive Lotus Elan and the all-important new Mazda MX-5, each of which has already been mentioned in this book. Both models are now looked upon as modern classics in their own right, yet are still temptingly affordable. So which one makes the most sense?

The Lotus boasts a certain exclusivity compared with the mass-selling Mazda, as well as styling that still turns heads to this day. Its fantastic chassis design meant incredible handling capabilities for the time, while the turbocharged 1.6-litre ex-Isuzu engine fitted to most examples led to terrific performance. A top speed of 219kmh (136mph) and a 0–100kmh (0–62mph) sprint time of just 6.5 seconds was thrilling stuff back then – and still provides serious entertainment now.

The best advice is to buy the finest Elan you can find for your money, with a low-ish mileage and – crucially – a complete service history. Get that right and you'll enjoy one of the most

entertaining sports cars to come out of Britain in the last few years of the twentieth century. It's just a shame the Elan didn't achieve greater success or a longer production run: Lotus called time after less than three years (though a further 400 examples were subsequently built in 1994) before the whole design and production rights ended up being sold to Kia.

All the models offered over the years by the likes of TVR, Reliant, and Lotus have been glassfibre in construction, usually with steel backbone chassis that – ideally – will have been galvanised to prevent future rust problems. Don't forget, though, to check the chassis carefully for signs of damage or corrosion, as well as the 'plastic' bodywork for evidence of cracks, crazing, poor repair work, drooping doors, and other typical problems.

Meanwhile, what about the Lotus Elan's most affordable new rival of the time, the Mazda MX-5? Well, what can we say? The 1989–98 Series I MX-5 has to rank as the most sensible modern classic money can buy. The fact that early examples are also extremely affordable these days is even better news. I mean, despite the value on offer, any well-sorted MX-5 will provide fun, sporty motoring with reliability, decent handling, lively

BELOW The concept of the proper MG sports car reappeared back in 1992 when the V8-engined RV8 took a bow. Just 2,000 were produced in total. *(MG Rover)*

performance, excellent build quality, longevity, and a whole lot more thrown in for nothing.

Compared with the classic sportsters of old, the first-generation MX-5 is refreshingly free of rust (though it still pays to check everywhere, as mentioned in the next chapter), impressively dependable, and a great long-term proposition. It's a relatively modern vehicle, and yet it still offers all the driver appeal of a traditional roadster – which is exactly what Mazda was determined to achieve during the model's development.

If a modern classic is your vehicle of choice, we can't praise the MX-5 too highly – so miss it off your own personal wish list at your peril. On sale in the UK and most of Europe from 1990 onwards, the Series I version is as impressive now as it's always been. But it's not the only classic from the '90s worthy of consideration.

The resurrection of MG as a builder of genuine sports car occurred in 1992, when the 3.9-litre V8-engined MG RV8 took a bow. In truth, this was little more than a rehash of the original MGB, albeit

BELOW The first all-new MG sports car in over 30 years, the mid-engined MG*F* caused quite a stir when it first appeared in '95, going on to enjoy considerable sales success. *(MG Rover)*

with a modified (and more muscular looking) bodyshell, extra power (190bhp) and, of course, uprated (but not necessarily updated) steering, suspension, and brakes. This was very much an 'old school' model intended only for limited production, which explains why the final RV8 was hand-finished as early as 1995, after a run of just 2,000 units. These days it makes a fantastic modern classic, combining nostalgic charm with modern-day performance. Just don't get caught out by its oh-so-1960s handling, will you?

What the RV8 did best, of course, was to pave the way for the next genuinely new MG sports car, the long-awaited MGF of 1995, the mid-engined two-seater created to give the Mazda MX-5 a run for its money. In many ways it succeeded, going on to achieve healthy sales throughout its lengthy life. The MGF may not have been quite as much fun to drive as its Japanese rival, but it still created a loyal following for itself among sports car enthusiasts delighted to see the MG badge properly back in action.

Whatever the age and type of classic you're buying, the principles involved in the process are generally quite similar – as are the potential pitfalls. *(Author)*

Buying, restoring, maintaining

So what makes a **classic?**

Is it age alone that transforms what was previously just a second-hand sports car into a desirable classic?

No, far from it. It's true that some of today's best-loved classic sports cars tend to come from earlier eras, when cars were simpler, designs were more individual, and the driving experience was rawer. But there's no 'cut-off date' for what makes a classic, even though it's only pre-1973 cars that (in the UK at least) are granted official Historic Vehicle status and are therefore eligible for free tax discs. In reality, the definition of a classic sports car is much less rigid than that.

Take, for example, the Series I Mazda MX-5, the mass-produced success story that brought the sports car world back to life at the end of the '80s. Some might argue it still isn't old enough to be considered a true classic. The majority of enthusiasts, however, would suggest this best-selling two-seater was such an influential design and such a trendsetter that its classic status is assured, irrespective of its age.

The obvious advice is to go for the sports car that most appeals to you (and can be found within your budget), and not worry about whether it's generally seen as a classic in its own right. You like it, you want it – does it matter what the rest of the world thinks?

Make sure, though, that with any car that's seen by some as a classic and by others as merely second-hand you're not paying over the odds for the privilege. Check what's being asked for similar examples elsewhere, and don't assume that just because you consider it a classic it's worth paying extra cash for. In any sector of the market, it's easy to get ripped off.

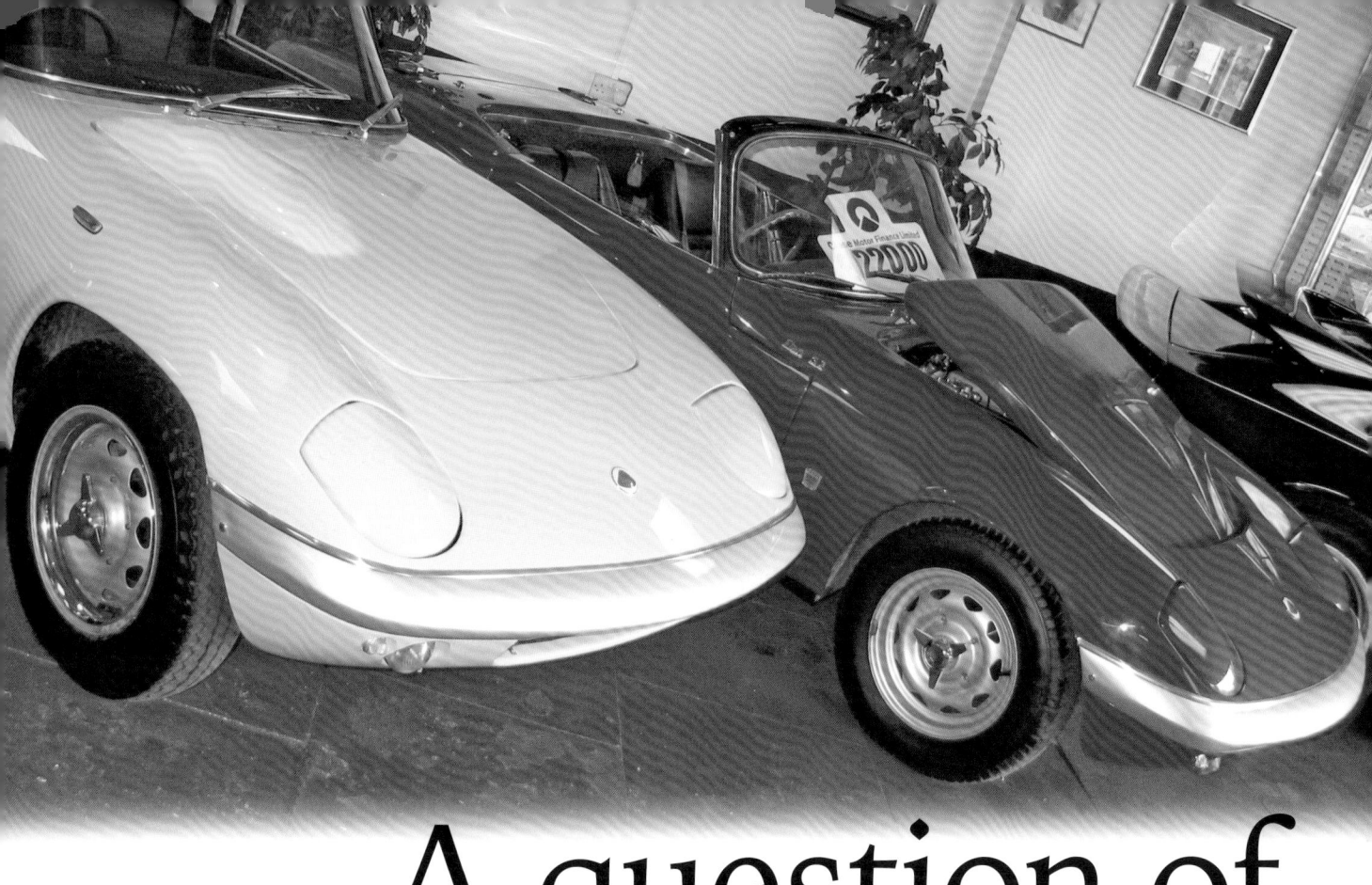

A question of
values

Placing a value on a classic sports car can be difficult. Any car under, say, ten years of age is easy enough to value via a used car price guide picked up from your local newsagents, but older vehicles can be trickier to value accurately.

Many classic car magazines do publish price guides for the most popular models, but these are sometimes less exact and less in-depth than you might be used to. They're useful as a starting point but shouldn't be taken too literally – particularly as the values of two seemingly similar models can sometime vary quite dramatically.

There are many factors to take into account when valuing any classic sports car. What are similar cars being advertised for elsewhere? How does the condition of this example compare with others? Has a top-quality restoration been carried out at great expense? Will the car need renovation or repair work in the near future? Is it a particularly rare or desirable specification? Has this example won any concours-type awards? The list goes on, but you get the idea.

Research is the key when considering any particular model of classic sports car – and that means scouring magazines and the Internet to compare asking prices, as well as chatting with owners and club members and asking their advice on the best derivative to go for and what you should expect to pay. Such advice will prove invaluable.

ABOVE Buying your sports car from a classic car specialist can sometimes be the most hassle-free direction to go in – depending on your budget, of course. *(Author)*

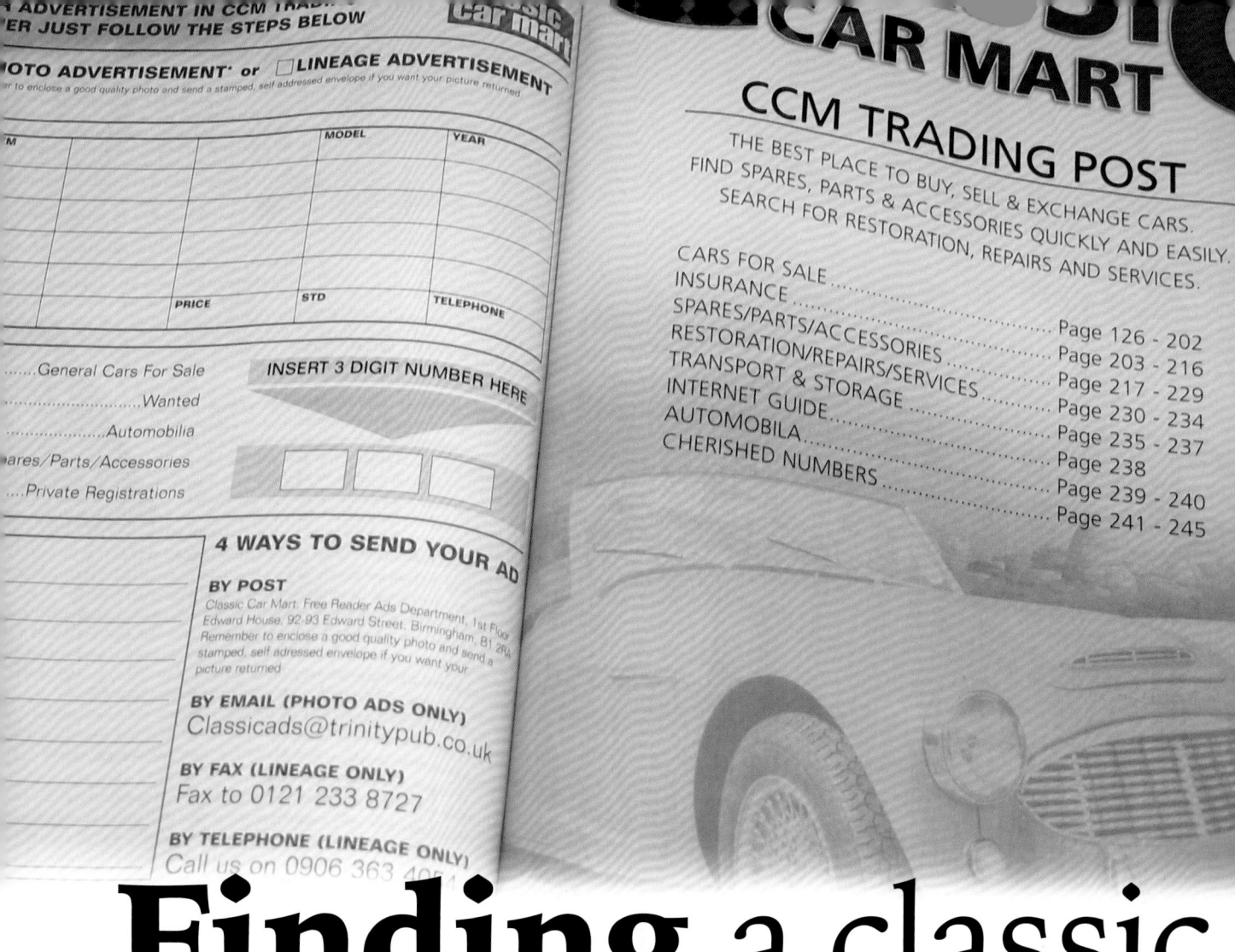

Finding a classic

When buying a classic sports car, you're again faced with another familiar dilemma: should you buy privately, should you head for your nearest classic car retailer, or should you consider bidding at a classic car auction? It's not a dissimilar situation to buying any used vehicle in this respect, and your final decision tends to come down to personal preference.

In Chapter Seven, we mentioned that buying a used sports car from a dealer can bring greater peace of mind, as it means added protection under the Sale of Goods Act. However, don't assume this is always the case with a classic car. Much depends on the claimed condition of the sports car in question, with some classic car specialists describing most of their vehicles as 'Projects' – which basically means no comeback if your car turns out to be in need of major work.

Most of the reputable classic car dealers are honest when describing their stock, which brings obvious reassurance. However, if the gearbox suddenly fails on a 30-year-old classic you've only owned for a fortnight, you won't necessarily have legal rights. It's an old vehicle and, as with any ageing consumer item, things can – and do – go wrong. A caring dealer may offer to contribute towards the cost or even get the car fixed for you; but this will be at his own discretion in most cases.

When buying a classic sportster privately or from a classic car auction, your rights – or lack of them – are pretty much as described in Chapter Seven. As ever, this is very much a case of Buyer Beware.

Restored or original?

Checking over a classic sports car demands the same thoroughness as when inspecting any used sportster, so I won't bother repeating myself unnecessarily. What is worth bearing in mind, though, is that the vast majority of classics on the market will have had some kind of restoration work carried out over the years

You need to ensure this has been done to a standard that's both acceptable to you and in keeping with the vendor's asking price.

The restoration work may have involved nothing more than a cosmetic respray, and maybe not even a complete one at that. Or it could have meant a complete rebuild, with brand new body panels, interior, chrome, and so on. It's important you chat with the vendor about exactly what has been carried out in the way of renovation, and that you're satisfied the work has been done to a good standard.

Have any replacement panels been fitted well, with even shut lines and neat welds? Are there any signs of poorly applied body filler (used by some unscrupulous owners to disguise rusted areas) beneath the fresh paintwork? Are any new panels of good enough quality if they're not from the original manufacturer? Is the respray a high quality one, with a smooth finish (free of any orange-peel effect, for example) and a depth to its shine? Has

ABOVE Has the rechroming been done well – assuming it's been done at all? Putting right poor quality work could end up costing you serious money. *(Author)*

any rechroming been carried out well, with no signs of ripples or flaking chrome? Has any reupholstery been done neatly, with original-style detailing and authentic looking material? How in-depth was the engine rebuild and are there any receipts to prove the work that's being claimed? How thorough was the complete mechanical overhaul, or will the car need some further attention at a later date? These are all questions you'll need answered if you're expected to pay full market value for a fully restored classic.

Happily, you needn't feel alone in your search. I touched on the subject of independent car inspections in Chapter Seven, and it's an option that's just as relevant in the classic market. In fact you have even more choice, as there are companies and qualified individuals specialising in

nothing but classic car inspections these days. Check out the advertisements in any national classic car magazine for details of the independent examiners closest to you.

Sometimes you'll come across a classic sports car for sale that's described by its vendor as 'totally original', and that can sound very tempting indeed. Does it mean, though, that there are jobs likely to be needed that have simply been neglected up until now? And if such originality is the result of long-term dry storage, you need to be sure that getting the car back on the road and in semi-regular use won't bring its own set of problems. Inactivity can be damaging, so a thorough mechanical overhaul may be an unexpected consequence of buying a car that's seen little use in recent years.

BELOW If your preference is for a classic sportster that has already been thoroughly restored, you should satisfy yourself that the work has been done to a high standard and is commensarate with the price you're paying for the car. (John Colley)

Restoration
projects

If you're even braver than that, of course, you might want to consider taking on a full-scale restoration project – although it's easy to get carried away with the romance of it all.

Cosy winter evenings spent tinkering with a few spanners, as a rusted hulk of sports car metal gradually gets transformed into a gleaming show-winner of a classic, all in the comfort of a centrally heated garage and surrounded by the finest tools and all the spare parts you could wish for…

Well, life isn't like that, sadly. You're far more likely to spend your evenings flat on your back on a freezing concrete garage floor, rain dripping through the roof, your fingers numb, your tool kit sadly inadequate, your language foul enough to

shock a shipbuilder, as you curse the day you ever bought the box of bits that sits before you, laughably described in the advert as an 'unfinished project'.

The completion of any restoration, of course, makes it all worthwhile. And it's a bit like childbirth, because no matter what pain you go through in the process, you'll probably go and do it all again a couple of years down the line.

Whether you're a restoration virgin or an old hand at rebuilds, it's vital that you choose a project that is within your capabilities. Most of us can't afford chequebook restorations (even if we wanted to), so we do much of the work ourselves. But we all have our limitations. Unless you're experienced with a MIG welder, should you really buy a classic sportster that's in need of major bodywork renovation? And if you don't know your torque wrench from your junior hacksaw, are you simply looking at the idea of a restoration through rose-tinted glasses?

ABOVE If you need to rely on professional help along the way, you'll need to incorporate this into your budget. Most single-marque specialists provide a decent service at competitive rates, though it pays to shop around. *(Author)*

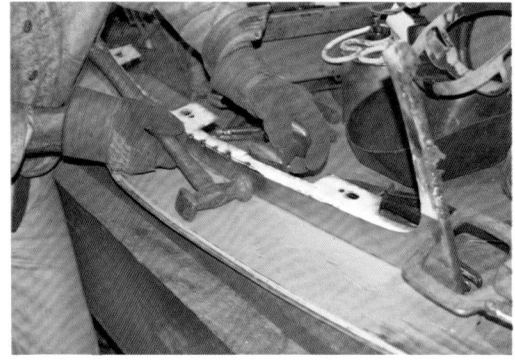

The term 'restoration project' can be applied to classic sports cars in wildly different states of disrepair, from an MoT failure that requires a couple of sills, a respray, and a few mechanical jobs to be made virtually perfect, to a box of bits that's claimed to be a Triumph TR4 but in reality looks more like the unwanted leftovers from a recent autojumble. In the case of the latter – or, indeed, any sports car that's not fully assembled when you inspect it – it is essential you're satisfied that the vast majority of components are actually there; even if they're not in good order, they will be invaluable when it comes to sourcing spares or having pattern parts made.

Your choice of make and model of sports car is very much a personal thing, but again you need to apply logic – and you need a realistic view of your own abilities and aspirations. For first-time classic restorers, the best advice is to choose a model for which there's excellent spares back-up from one-make specialists. Otherwise you could spend huge amounts of time trying to locate obscure parts,

commissioning patterns, and generally getting very depressed by the whole project. Pick an old favourite like an MGB, Midget, or Triumph Spitfire and you can literally build up a shopping list of items you'll need, together with detailed prices courtesy of your local friendly specialist. You'll then have a much better idea of what the entire project is likely to cost before you get too involved.

While we're on the subject of budgeting, it's essential that you make sure you can afford to see the project through before you buy the car. An ultra-cheap 'box of bits' sports car may seem a bargain, but if it's going to cost you several thousand more to get the thing back on the road, is it really worth it? You could end up spending much, much more than the car is worth simply getting it to a roadworthy condition.

When budgeting don't underestimate the cost of anything. Whatever you reckon it will set you back (whether it's having a front wing fitted or carrying out a brake and steering rebuild), it's bound to cost more: one job inevitably leads to another, extra work is found to be required, and suddenly you've got bills to pay that are twice as much as you anticipated. There's no finer way of ending up either broke or in the divorce courts, as plenty of experienced restorers will confirm.

Take your time, choose your make and model carefully, research the spares situation before you buy, make a detailed list of your anticipated expenditure (then add some more), talk to other owners, analyse your own capabilities with honesty … do all this and you're in with a fighting chance of sports car restoration success.

The **hard work** begins

Classifieds sections of magazines are littered with classic sports cars described as 'unfinished projects'. Most of the time, that's because an enthusiast has started a restoration, only to lose interest or motivation partway through.

Much of that, though, is down to a lack of planning, and it's at this crucial early stage that forward-planning needs to be carefully carried out, to save you from heartache in the months and years ahead.

So, assuming that the classic sports car you've bought is to be the subject of a thorough, in-depth rebuild rather than a 'rolling restoration', what you do next is critical to how the entire project will turn out. It's all too easy to dash into your garage next Saturday, start ripping bits off the car and feel satisfied that the strip-down process is well under way. But this is where the problems start. A year or two from now, when you need to actually start replacing those bits and pieces or find substitutes, you won't know where you've put them, where they came from, or how they're fitted. You might think you'll remember at the time, but you won't.

You need to tackle the task as though it were a military operation. You want to start stripping parts off the car? Fine. But each and every item should be carefully removed, cleaned, labelled, and stored away for future use or for replacement at a later date.

The storage of parts is vital to straightforward reassembly later on. Don't just assume that throwing items into the corner of the garage or piling them up on shelves is the answer. Try to establish some kind of logical storage system, with separate areas devoted to exterior trim, interior trim, steering, braking, engine bay, and so on, covering all separate areas you can think of. A properly disassembled car will take up a large amount of space, which is obviously a bit of a luxury; but this kind of forward planning and detailing will save you huge amounts of time later on.

The extent of the strip-down depends on the extent of the restoration work required. You may be intending to strip your sports car project to a rolling shell, prior to full-scale bodywork repairs, a bare metal respray and full reassembly using nearly all new components. Or you might just want to remove all the trim and 'minor' mechanicals, leaving much of the car intact but allowing you to tackle more localised body repairs and a rather less thorough respray. The choice is yours. Either way, though, apply the same logical system to your stripping process and you'll be thankful later on.

Getting it running

Assuming your newly acquired classic sports car doesn't need full-scale restoration but will require a good 'going over' before it sets tyres on tarmac again, you'll doubtless be tempted to get it up and running as soon as possible – particularly if it hasn't been run for some time and you've only got the vendor's word for the fact that the engine was 'fine last time I started it'. But, as ever, caution is the keyword.

BELOW If your newly acquired classic sportster hasn't been run in a long time, you'll need to carry out various checks and tasks before turning the key. *(Andrew Noakes)*

Don't be tempted to just connect up a battery and turn the key, hoping for the best. Almost certainly you'll be doing more harm than good. If the car has stood for some time, the fuel in the tank could have deteriorated; moisture could have got into the engine oil; internal components could have rusted together; coolant could have drained away.

The answer is to go through the pre-starting process step by step. Try turning the engine by hand to make sure it's not seized (which presumably you'll have ascertained before you bought the car…). Assuming all is well, you'll need to drain the old engine oil from the sump and replace with new; drain the coolant and fill the system with a water/antifreeze mixture; replace the plugs and points; fit new plug leads if necessary; check the condition and working order of the condenser, the distributor/cap, the coil and so on; make sure a healthy battery is fully charged; and then you might just about be ready to try starting your future pride and joy for the first time.

This stage is also an excellent opportunity to carry out research into spares for your particular vehicle, using classic car magazines and the Internet as essential guides. Try to establish which companies specialise in your model, making sure you get in touch to establish contact and to find out exactly what they offer. They'll be able to advise on parts availability and costs, as well as various weak points and 'suspect' areas of the model in question.

The same applies to clubs, whose members are a goldmine of helpful advice and information. Tackling a restoration without being a member of the relevant club is like going camping without a tent, so check out some of the major clubs we've listed in Appendix B.

Bodywork nightmares?

It's a fact of life that most sports car restorations revolve around the rebuilding of bodywork. That's not to say that engine reconditioning and mechanical overhauls are in any way minor issues. Far from it. But the main reason for restoration in the first place is, in so many cases, because the car's bodywork has finally succumbed to old age, road salt, and the ravages of rust.

Assuming the classic you've bought is of traditional steel construction (whether of monocoque design or featuring a separate chassis), it's unlikely to have experienced 20, 30, 40 or more years of active life without suffering some kind of body deterioration. If you're lucky it might be just a few replacement body panels that are required; or if you're like thousands of other enthusiasts, you'll find yourself with a stripped bodyshell on your hands (well, on axle stands) that needs structural repairs underneath, panel replacements, extra strengthening, and a whole lot more.

How much of this work is done by you depends on your own skills with a MIG welder. If they're limited, you'll find professionals willing to help – but have you costed the work and can you actually afford it? You might find a mobile welder who charges a very competitive hourly rate, but this could still add up to a seriously large sum of money as time goes by. And you also need to ensure his work is not simply to 'MoT standard' but

ABOVE Fitting new trim after a respray? That's great; but you should have had a trial run before any paint was applied, just to make sure everything fits well and your fresh new paintwork won't get damaged. *(Author)*

RIGHT Rust like this will be familiar to anybody who's about to tackle a restoration. You should be aware of the full extent of the damage before you buy the car. *(Paul Hardiman)*

RIGHT At all stages of the restoration, your car should be properly secured on axle stands rather than supported by jacks. Your life could depend on it. *(Paul Hardiman)*

RIGHT Cutting away old rust is the only way to stop the rot. Can you buy replacement panels for your particular sports car, though? Find out before you make a start. *(Paul Hardiman)*

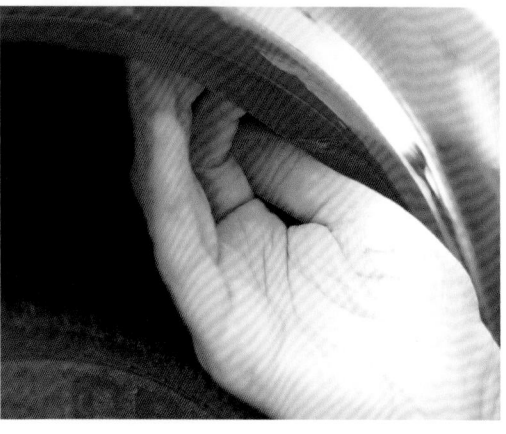

RIGHT If you can't get hold of the brand new replacement panel (or section) that you require, it might be possible to create your own particularly if it's a simple shape, as shown here. *(Andrew Noakes)*

is actually worthy of a classic sports car such as yours.

There'll inevitably be garages local to you who could carry out repairs, but again at a cost. And you've then got the hassle of getting a stripped and relatively immobile bodyshell to them.

If you're happy with your own standards of welding, there's the option of doing all the bodywork repairs yourself, as countless owners and enthusiasts do. It's all part of the fun to so many of them. But, as with any restoration task, you must ensure that safety is your top priority.

Whenever you're working underneath your car, it must be secured on proper axle stands – don't *ever* trust a car jack to hold the weight. You must also ensure that it's safe to weld where you intend to weld, that it's not placing anybody else in any danger, that you're wearing protective clothing and a welding mask, and that there's somebody standing by to help with any problems.

The style of the repairs depends on your budget, your requirements, and the state of the car. Is it best to repair an original panel or fit a replacement, for example? That depends on how bad the corrosion is. If half the panel is eaten away, a replacement is usually the most cost effective and most satisfactory choice – assuming it's available. However, if the rust is fairly localised, there's no reason why sections cannot be cut away, replaced with new metal, and the job completed with old-fashioned lead loading or more modern body filler for a decent finish.

No matter how good a welder you are, you're probably not one of the world's greatest sprayers. Few of us are. For most of us, the final respray is one area where we admit defeat and call in the professionals. It can be pricey, of course. But you tend to get what you pay for, so some sort of a compromise should be achievable between your requirements on the one hand and your available budget on the other. And at least while your car is away at the spray shop, it gives you time to search for all that new, replacement trim you've been promising yourself, right? Wrong!

To get your gleaming new bodyshell back from the spray shop and then start fitting trim for the first time is foolhardy in the extreme. Before any paint is applied, all trim should be trial-fitted to ensure there are no problems. It's amazing how seemingly similar looking items of trim for exactly the same year and model of car can vary so much, but it's true. Don't take anything for granted.

Your restoration project will be making good progress by now, and it's at this stage that you'll be pleased you carried out all that earlier forward planning.

Protection for the future

Once your sports car restoration (whether that means a full-scale rebuild or relatively minor cosmetics) is complete, you might think all the hard work's over with. Your beloved classic is reassembled and you can sit back and ponder exactly what you've achieved. It's sailed through its MoT test, it's sporting a nice new tax disc, and it's fully insured. All in all, you deserve a pat on the back for a job well done.

The worst thing you can do, though, is jump straight into the driver's seat and embark upon a few years of classic motoring. Not because we're recommending you hide your classic away in a garage, never to see the light of day unless the weather forecasters predict a year-long drought; but simply because this is the time for carrying out some preventative maintenance to help prevent rust taking a hold once more.

First job is to make sure your newly restored bodyshell is protected from the elements. Even if you don't intend using the car all year round, there are very few garages (if any) that are totally free of condensation and damp. Don't underestimate the power of rust. Even when sat in a garage, a classic sports car can be deteriorating before your eyes, as condensation takes hold of chassis members, doors, sills, and just about every other section of steel. And much of the damage happens from the inside out, so by the time you can see what's going on it's too late.

The answer is to ensure that all welded joints are properly sealed prior to spraying; that vulnerable underside areas (such as inner wheel arches, inner sills, floorpans and so on) are coated with a thin layer of underbody sealant, the product marketed by Waxoyl being particularly recommended for its elasticity; and that all box sections (chassis members and so on) and relevant panels (doors, sills, et al) are liberally treated with Waxoyl itself – or any similar product – to ensure that any moisture cannot find its way into cracks and corners and start the whole rusting process all over again.

It's particularly important to ensure that all inner areas of steel are treated in this way, which means inside the sills, inside all box sections, and inside the doors. Take your time, be ultra-vigilant with your rustproofing, and the long-term benefits will be enormous.

ABOVE Following any restoration, it's imperative you carry out thorough rust-proofing to prevent premature deterioation in the future. Even when stored in a garage, dampness in the air can cause problems aplenty. You don't want all that hard work going to waste… *(iStockphoto)*

Cleaning and storage

To keep your classic sports car's paintwork at its best (particularly when it comes to newly sprayed areas), you need to ensure it's regularly waxed using any of the popular brands that offer good protection without being too abrasive.

Autoglym's range of polishes and cleaners is particularly recommended by the author, with excellent water repellent qualities in all the tests we've carried out on our own vehicles.

The same goes for chrome, too, much of which will either have been replaced or replated during restoration. Using a quality chrome cleaner/polish will help it to keep its lustre. During the winter months, it's a good idea to smear a thin layer of Waxoyl across chrome surfaces, whether or not you intend using your car all year round; it may not look too tidy afterwards, but it will keep garage condensation or road salt (depending on the car's circumstances) from damaging the chrome all over again. The Waxoyl is then easily removed once spring arrives, using nothing more than polish or even white spirit.

The actual storage of any classic sports car can have a huge effect on how it maintains its good looks over the next few years. It's all very well taking your vehicle off the road during the winter to protect it from the ravages of road salt, snow, and ice, but standing in a damp, condensation-lined garage can be just as bad. Mechanically it can be even worse, with brakes and clutch more likely to seize, rubbers more liable to perishing, and all moving components bound to suffer. Regular usage of your classic is an ideal antidote to such problems, but only if you carry out the precautions I outlined earlier.

Assuming your garage is as dry as can be expected, your car may well benefit from a good quality dust cover, with most of the popular brands being advertised each month in various classic car magazines. But for the ultimate in protection, there's also the range of Carcoon products available, allowing you to store your treasured sports car in its own 'bubble' through which dry air is circulated. The result is a total lack of condensation and, inevitably, little or no chance of any new corrosion taking hold. It's the ultimate way of avoiding all damage-inducing moisture.

Restoring any classic car from a wreck to a potential show winner – or even just to 'daily user' status – is incredibly hard work and should not be undertaken lightly. However, by the time you get to this stage you'll be fully ready to enjoy your machine on the finest roads you can find. And that's what it's all about: fun and enjoyment.

Whether you've carried out your own restoration or you bought your classic with all the hard work already done, take your time to ensure you maintain the vehicle properly and keep it in tip-top condition. Oh, and if you've had major work carried out that's increased its market value, don't forget to increase the agreed value of its classic car insurance policy; you need to ensure your car is properly protected at all times.

OPPOSITE Whether your classic's paintwork is original or fairly recent, keeping it protected and well polished should be part of your maintenance regime, even if your car is stored away during the worst of the winter weather. *(Autoglym)*

BELOW Keeping all chrome and metallic areas polished will help to reduce damage caused by moisture and pollution. Wire wheels are fiddly to clean but look superb when in excellent condition. *(Author)*

Classic
car **insurance**

ABOVE Classic car
insurance is available
these days for most
sports cars over ten or
fifteen years of age,
and is often
dramatically more
affordable than a
conventional policy.
(Porsche)

Actually, the many benefits of
classic car insurance can be
another bonus of choosing an
older sports car over merely a
second-hand one. And, happily,
classic insurers have become
much more open-minded in
recent years, with many models
that were previously ignored now
being eligible for cover.

The principle of classic car insurance is simple.
You insure your sports car for an agreed amount,
the stipulation usually being that you don't exceed
a pre-arranged annual mileage, you keep the car
garaged at night, you don't use it as your everyday
transport, you have a reasonably trouble-free
driving history, and you're over the age of either 21
or 25 (depending on the make and model you're
trying to insure). The insurer knows your car is fairly
low risk because you're a classic car enthusiast
who won't drive as recklessly as, say, a 17-year-
old in a modified Fiesta. And because you'll
probably only be using your classic during the
summer months and generally at weekends, the
risks are far lower than for somebody who drives

20,000 miles a year in their family car. Classic car owners tend to treat their machines with care and respect, and the insurers know this – which is why it's possible in many cases to get a surprisingly low premium quote.

There was a time when a car had to be at least 20 years old to be considered for classic insurance. In the UK now, though, there are many insurers happy to insure far younger sports cars on a classic-type policy, with the same limited mileage and agreed value conditions. This means that many Mazda MX-5s, MG*F*s, Lotus Elans, MG RV8s and other relatively 'modern' classics can now enjoy the benefits of proper classic car insurance cover.

The number of insurers providing classic cover has grown immensely in the last few years, and a glance at any British classic car magazine will show most of them advertising their policies. Which company and policy you choose may be as straightforward as opting for the cheapest quote, but it's always worth bearing in mind the various terms and conditions, as well as certain benefits offered with some policies.

Does the classic insurance policy you're about to agree to offer breakdown cover as well, for example? (Many do, and it can be cheaper than having separate cover arranged elsewhere.) Does it offer a salvage buy-back facility in the unfortunate event of your beloved sports car being written-off in an accident? (You might want to retrieve your car and put the insurance payout towards rebuilding it yourself.) Does it offer a guaranteed agreed value that reflects what it would cost to replace your car if the worst happens? Does it offer European cover in case you're tempted to head overseas on a classic touring holiday? Make sure you choose a classic policy that suits your own particular needs rather than one that slightly undercuts every other quote you've been given.

Classic car insurance can be a superb way of bringing down the cost of one of today's biggest motoring expenses. As ever, though, be prepared – and make sure you get a reasonable number of quotes for the classic sports car you're interested in buying, so that you know what to expect before you actually take the plunge.

ABOVE Even a modern classic like an MGF or Mazda MX-5 can now be insured on a classic car policy. Keep your annual mileage realistic, your car garaged and your driving license clean and you should find yourself paying a very realistic premium. *(MG Rover)*

10

Add-ons
& upgrades

**You want to upgrade
and improve your
sports car? You're not
alone, whether that
means cosmetic
improvements or some
kind of performance
boost. *(Nissan)***

The **options**

You've just bought the sports car of your dreams (or at least the one that you most like within your budget) and now you're keen to give it that 'something extra' compared with all the others out there. That might mean some cosmetic mods, or a performance upgrade, or both. But where do you start?

BELOW The fitment of a performance air filter from the likes of K&N can be simple, inexpensive, and effective – a great way of acquiring a couple of extra brake-horsepower. *(K&N)*

Well, you only have to glance through any of the classic, sports, and performance car magazines, or do an Internet search under your favourite make and model, to realise there's no shortage of specialists around willing to help improve your sportster. And whether that means an engine chip for extra brake-horsepower, a full-on body kit for head-turning looks, or a suspension upgrade guaranteed to ensure even firmer, roll-free cornering, you'll find plenty of companies anxious to attract your custom.

Among the simplest and most affordable upgrades available for most sports cars are performance air filters and aftermarket exhaust systems, the combination of which could add a handful of extra brake-horsepower to your car's output, as well as aiding its sheer responsiveness. But what if you want to go further?

If it's a modern sports car we're talking about, you could always have your engine re-chipped – plenty of owners do. But what exactly does this entail? In simple terms, it's all to do with the fuel injection and engine management systems. The new, upgraded chip fits into your car's ECU and basically 'ups' the fuelling and the ignition timing. This means extra power, a more instant throttle response, and better acceleration, particularly effective in the case of a turbocharged sports car.

No problems there, then. Except it's not quite as simple as that. Any reputable specialist who's chipping your car will reset the CO level and raise the fuel pressure to cope with it all, as well as ensuring an excellent state of tune for the engine. The car will then be put on a rolling road and run carefully up to the desired power level. But less sympathetic treatment could cause serious damage to your engine. Bear all this in mind when shopping around for a chipping specialist, and at all costs avoid anyone down the pub who says they can 'do it for fifty quid'.

Older sports cars – and particularly the most popular classic models – can benefit from extra power simply by fitting higher-spec carburettors from the likes of Webcon (check out the company's website at www.webcon.co.uk), suppliers of upgraded Weber carburettor kits for a wide range of classics. Improved carburation and better breathing can help even the most aged of well-maintained engines to gain extra power and offer improved performance.

Brakes and suspension

Any major increase in power brings the predicament of whether your standard braking and suspension systems can cope – and there's no all-encompassing answer to this. If in any doubt, seek advice from a specialist.

If an improved braking system is what's needed, you might consider drilled, vented, or grooved new discs. The idea behind these is to aid brake cooling, repel water and moisture, and keep the pads themselves as clean as possible. The difference with vented discs is that, to look at, they resemble two discs stuck together but with a gap between that fills with cold air. Many of today's high-performance sports cars already have vented discs fitted as standard, though rarely of the drilled type.

All these disc designs work extremely well. After all, water being constantly forced against discs and pads must have somewhere to go. Grooved and drilled discs allow for this, thus preventing the water from ruining the compound of the brake pads and leading to brake fade or outright failure. It's all damn clever stuff.

For the ultimate in braking upgrades, you'll need to add top-quality four-pot callipers (for extreme cooling under very hard braking) to your list of requirements. Or you could always opt for something like an AP Racing Performance Brake Kit, available for a growing list of models and consisting of a pair of vented front discs, lightweight alloy anodised mounting bells, four-pot alloy callipers, purpose-designed calliper mounting brackets, and Mintex high-performance brake pads. That's quite a package – but it also comes with quite a price tag.

Braking upgrades are a fine idea. But take it too far and you'll find the new braking force passing

extra stress onto your car's anti-roll bar bushes, steering joints and bushes, suspension bushes and so on. All these areas will also need uprating if you go too far with your brakes. Then you need to ask yourself whether your dampers are stiff enough and your car low enough to cope with the extra braking. And it's a similar story with the spec of your tyres.

The moral of the story? Upgrade your brakes and suspension sensibly, don't go over the top and end up ruining your car.

ABOVE If you dramatically increase your sports car's performance or braking capabilities, you'll be well advised to look at upgrading its suspension, too. (Author)

The **wheel** thing

The same advice applies equally to wheels and tyres, as any major changes here can have knock-on effects elsewhere. So once you've set your heart on a set of shiny new alloys, what's the magic formula when it comes to deciding which size to go for? Should you stick with standard width or go all the way and have absolute monsters fighting to escape from under your arches?

BELOW A set of alloy wheels can be a major investment – but what a transformation! *(Mazda)*

There's no hard and fast rule when it comes to sizing. For the ultimate in one-upmanship, plenty of folk go for the biggest they can squeeze in without fouling their wheelarches. A lot of it's down to personal preference.

The starting point is inevitably a good aftermarket wheel retailer who can tell you instantly what the biggest wheel is that can sensibly be used on your machine. They know their stuff – they've been into modded cars for years and they're worth listening to. But is it always best to go for the biggest sizing? Well, not necessarily. The bigger and fatter the wheels and tyres, the more likely they are to follow track lines in an uneven road surface, which could mean you're fighting with your steering wheel a lot more than before.

And while fitting fatter rims will, in most cases, improve your car's roadholding, there's a point beyond which any such benefits cease. If 16-inch wheels result in the ultimate grip and handling, is there any point going for 17s just to be one up on the 'competition'? Well, that's your call. Just don't expect an automatic improvement in roadholding that corresponds with each bigger size.

If you're intent on fitting a monstrous set of rims, it's also worth investigating the effects on your particular sports car's brakes and steering before actually taking the plunge. And that's why any modifications you're likely to carry out in the future need to be planned carefully.

Think about what you're trying to achieve, study the various ways of getting there, look at the costs involved, and talk to as many fellow owners and specialists as you can. Every modification you carry out will almost certainly affect something else on your car, so the order in which you carry them out is vital. Get it right, though, and you'll have a great-looking sports car to be proud of, and a machine even more rewarding to drive than its maker intended.

One thing to bear in mind when fitting expensive new wheels, however, is to ensure your insurance company is aware of the change. We cover the subject of insurance in more depth elsewhere, but it's worth emphasising here: you are legally obliged to inform your insurance company of any change to your car's specification, and that includes the fitment of non-standard wheels. Failure to do this could bring unexpected problems in the event of a future claim.

Uprated Brake Discs

arch

Cars

line Catalogues

3B
3A
prite Midget Early
prite Midget Late
GF
riumph TR2-4A
riumph TR5-6-250
pitfire
IX5
lassic Mini
lew Mini

Downloadable PDFs

Classic Mini
MG T-Type 1936-'55
MGA 1955-'62

Heavy braking can tax even disc brakes and, if they are proving inadequate, we supply grooved & cross-drilled discs that run considerably cooler than standard, ideal for really hard driving or competition use.

Description	Application	Part No.	Price	Qty Rqd	Qty	
DISCS, Brake, Uprated (Grooved) MORE INFO Note: Pair	MGB	BTB387G	£79.96 €121.54	0	0	+ AC
DISCS, Brake, Uprated (X-Drilled) Note: Pair	MGB	DBD101	NLS	0	0	+ A
DISC, Brake, Uprated (X-Drilled) Note: Single	MGB V8	DBD102	£71.75 €109.06	0	0	+ A
Brake, Uprated (X-Drilled)		DBD103	£69.65	0	0	+

Classic modifications

What, though, if you're the proud owner of an older classic sports car – perhaps one of the more popular models from the 1950s, '60s, or '70s? Is it possible to carry out sensible modifications without spoiling the retro feel of the car? And what will it do to the vehicle's value in the long term?

Opinion is divided, with many traditionalists suggesting that all classics should remain exactly as they left the factory, even down to original-spec crossply tyres. But the tide has been turning since the mid-1990s, when increasing numbers of enthusiasts realised the benefits of modifying their classics to cope with modern traffic conditions – which usually meant improved suspension, uprated brakes, or simply some extra power.

The trend has evolved, and nowadays there's quite a following for modified classics of all types, with magazines available specialising in the scene. It's had the knock-on effect that, among single-marque classic car specialists, there's now a wider range of off-the-shelf upgrades available than ever

ABOVE The most popular classic sports cars now have modifications readily available 'off the shelf'. Check out a few specialists' websites to see what's out there for your make and model. Uprated brake discs for an MGB, anyone? *(Author)*

Internet to quickly realise what's available for your particular make and model of classic sportster.

So whether it's a front-disc brake conversion for an Austin-Healey Sprite, a five-speed gearbox kit for an MGB, or even a V8 engine transplant for a Triumph TR7, you'll find specialists on the scene ready and willing to help. As for any criticism from the purists of this world … well, it's your car and it's up to you what you do with it. The best advice? Ensure the modifications are in keeping with both the vehicle and what you're trying to achieve and you should be pleased with the end results; be sensible, don't go too far, and you'll end up with a usefully enhanced sports car that hasn't lost its classic feel. As ever, though, make sure you do your homework first.

As for the effect on vehicle value, this can vary depending on the make and model in question – and, of course, the quality of the modifications. A badly modified classic will always suffer value-wise; but a sporting classic that's had a series of sympathetic, good quality, highly effective upgrades carried out can be seen as more desirable in the eyes of many potential buyers, and therefore worth more. Even so, any increase in value is unlikely to cover what you spent on the modifications, so bear this in mind before spending large sums of cash.

ABOVE How do you feel about major modifications to a classic car? It's a growing scene, with V8 conversions for MGs being a perennial favourite among enthusiasts. *(Author)*

before, which makes sourcing and fitting the modifications easier than ever. You only need to talk to fellow club members, scour the specialist magazines, or carry out some research on the

RIGHT Period accessories have always been popular with classic sports car owners, with boot racks, wire wheels, and badge bars among the sought-after items. *(Author)*

And finally...

We're back to the thorny old subject of insurance, and whether your sportster is completely standard or highly modified, you need to make sure you've got adequate insurance cover arranged.

This isn't necessarily as straightforward as you might think, although the situation has improved over the last few years. It's not so long ago that most mainstream insurers wouldn't consider offering cover on a 'grey import' Mazda Miata (Japanese-spec MX-5), for example. Happily, though, they've been forced to adapt to market changes and, anxious not to lose business, most will now insure the kind of Japanese sports cars that were previously considered taboo.

Do be aware, though, that even a fairly modest 'grey import' will be required to have a Thatcham-approved immobiliser fitted (and your insurer would need proof of this via a fitter's certificate) before most insurance companies will offer cover. And when it comes to the actual premium, you'll find most 'grey imports' will cost anywhere between 25 and 40 per cent extra to insure, as well as incurring

a higher compulsory excess. Bear this in mind when comparing policies offered by different companies.

It's a similar situation when trying to insure any sports car that's been altered from its standard specification. At first, it may seem tempting not to admit to your car having been 'chipped' or your suspension and braking systems having being uprated. But, again, if you're unfortunate enough to have an accident and any such modifications are discovered by an assessor, it could make your entire insurance policy null and void – and you won't receive a penny.

Even fairly basic modifications like an aftermarket set of alloys should be declared to your insurer when arranging cover. You may pay a little extra for your policy, but at least you'll know your car and its expensive new wheels are adequately covered should the worst ever happen. If you're spending a serious amount of cash on improving, upgrading, or modifying your car, the last thing you should be cutting back on is your insurance. It just doesn't make sense.

Once that's sorted, though, you're ready for the off. And ready to discover that life with a sports car – whether new, used, or classic – can be fun, fulfilling, and dramatically more interesting than when you drove around in that dull old hatchback. It's time to enjoy yourself.

ABOVE If you're the proud owner of a modified or upgraded sportster, have you bothered to inform your insurance company of the changes? Your policy could be null and void if you haven't. *(Alfa Romeo)*

Sports car specialists

This is a selection of the specialists catering for the classic and modern sports car scenes at the time of writing. Companies are UK-based unless otherwise stated. If telephoning them from outside the UK, remember to cancel the '0' from the standard dialling code and replace with the '0044' international dialling code.

Space restrictions mean we can't list every specialist for every make and model of sports car; this list will, however, give a flavour of the kind of support that's out there.

ALFA ROMEO

Betacar
Tel: 01535 275560
Website: www.betacar.co.uk

Clovertech
Tel: 0208 470 7809
Website: www.clovertechuk.com

DTR European Sports Cars
Tel: 0208 878 6078
Website: www.dtrsports.com

TMC Alfas
Tel: 01305 260091
Website: www.thamesmotorcompany.co.uk

ASTON MARTIN

Andre Bloom
Tel: 01543 480868
Email: sales@astonmartin-gb.com

Aston Workshop
Tel: 01207 233525
Website: www.aston.co.uk

Byron International
Tel: 01737 244567
Website: www.allastonmartin.com

Desmond J. Smail
Tel: 0207 985 0111
Website: www.djsmail.co.uk

Nicholas Mee & Company
Tel: 0208 741 8822
Website: www.nicholasmee.co.uk

AUSTIN-HEALEY

Chiltern Classics
Tel: 0118 932 1708
Mobile: 07768 323466

Frogeye Spares Company (Sprite MkI)
Tel: 01885 400791
Website: www.frogeyespares.co.uk

Rawles Classic Healeys
Tel: 01420 23212
Website: www.austinhealeyspecialists.co.uk

CATERHAM SEVEN

Redline Components
Tel: 01883 346515
Website: www.redlinecomponents.co.uk

The 7 Workshop
Tel: 01992 470480
Email: info@7workshop.com

UK Sports Cars
Tel: 01227 728190
Website: www.uksportscars.com

Woodcote Sports Cars
Tel: 0208 641 9897
Website: www.woodcotesportscars.com

CLASSIC SPORTS CAR SALES (GENERAL)

Alan Carrington Classic & Sports Cars
Tel: 01732 870331
Website: www.alancarrington.com

Avro Motor Cars
Tel: 01932 352220
Website: www.avromotorcars.com

Beaulieu Garage
Tel: 01590 612999
Website: www.beaulieugarage.co.uk

Bespoke Selection
Tel: 01242 248777
Website: www.bespokeselection.co.uk

Bocking Garage
Tel: 01535 642085
Website: www.bockinggarage.co.uk

Bristol Classic & Sports Cars
Tel: 01275 342999
Website: www.bcandsc.co.uk

Californian Connection
Tel: 01335 300312
Website: www.apincorporated.com

Camberley Marine & Sports Cars
Tel: 01252 612245
Website: www.cms-gb.com

Chelsea Cars
Tel: 0208 870 9977
Website: www.chelseacars.com

Cheshire Classics
Tel: 01270 886134
Email: damon.milnes@virgin.net

Classic & Sports For Sale
Tel: 01920 830107
Website: www.classicandsportsforsale.co.uk

Classic Chrome
Tel: 0208 876 8171
Website: www.classic-chrome.co.uk

Cleevewood Garage
Tel: 0117 956 7144
Website: www.allsportscars.co.uk

Epping Motor Company
Tel: 01277 365415
Website: www.eppingmotorcompany.com

European Classic Cars
Tel: 01793 812266
Website: www.europeanclassiccars.co.uk

European Collectibles (USA)
Tel: (001) 949 650 4718
Website: www.europeancollectibles.com

Grundy Mack Classic Cars
Tel: 01944 758000
Website: www.grundymack.com

Hewitts
Tel: 0161 434 2731
Website: www.hewittsclassiccars.co.uk

Jojami Classics
Tel: 0208 500 8080
Website: www.myclassiccar.co.uk

Marksdanes
Tel: 01749 830812
Website: www.marksdanes.com

Mercury Classic Cars
Tel: 01333 320158
Website: www.mercuryclassiccars.com

Mike Abbas
Tel: 01257 470034
Website: www.mikeabbasclassiccars.co.uk

Modern Motoring
Tel: 01803 522828
Website: www.modernmotoring.co.uk

Moto-Build
Tel: 01784 477477
Website: www.moto-build.co.uk

Neal Barron Classic Cars
Tel: 01606 884342
Website: www.nealbarron.com

Nutley Sports & Prestige Centre
Tel: 01825 713388
Website: www.nutleysports.co.uk

Oselli
Tel: 01993 849610
Website: www.oselli.com

Percival Motor Company
Tel: 01622 851841
Website: www.percivalmotorco.co.u

PK Sports & Collectors' Cars
Tel: 01275 856168
Website: www.pksports-collectorscars.co.u

Sherwood Restorations
Tel: 01636 812700
Website: www.sherwoodrestorations.co.uk

Specialized Vehicle Solutions
Tel: 0161 789 0504
Website: svs-ltd.com

Titty Ho Motor Company
Tel: 01933 622206
Website: www.tittyhomotorco.com

Unicorn Motor Company
Tel: 01963 363353
Website: www.unicornmotor.com

VSOC (The Netherlands)
Tel: (0031) 252 218 980
Website: www.vsoc.nl

FERRARI

The Ferrari Centre
Tel: 07000 360355
Website: www.theferraricentre.co.uk

Forza 288
Tel: 01425 273682
Website: www.forza288.com

Foskers
Tel: 07000 355355
Website: www.foskers.com

Joe Macari Performance Cars
Tel: 0208 870 9007
Website: www.joemacari.com

FIAT

DTR European Sports Cars
Tel: 0208 878 6078
Website: www.dtrsports.com

JAGUAR

Clarkes (XJ-S specialist)
Tel: 01435 863800
Website: www.clarkesjaguar.co.uk

Coventry Auto Components (XK parts)
Tel: 02476 471217
Website: www.xk-parts.co.uk

David Kelly Car Dismantlers
Tel: 01978 843253
Website: www.davidkellycars.co.uk

David Manners
Tel: 0121 544 4444
Website: www.davidmanners.co.uk

Hollygrove Jaguar
Tel: 01425 477000
Website: www.hollygrove-jaguar.co.uk

Hyper Engineering
Tel: 01844 278481
Email: hyperxjs@aol.com

JD Classics
Tel: 01621 879579
Website: www.jdclassics.co.uk

Ken Jenkins Jaguar Spares
Tel: 01909 733209
Email: ukjag@hotmail.com

RM&J Smith (E-Type specialist)
Tel: 01270 820885
Email: rmj@rmjsmith.fsnet.co.uk

Terry's Jaguar Parts (USA)
Tel: (001) 618 439 4444
Website: www.terrysjag.com

Woodmanton Classics
Tel: 01885 410396
Website: www.woodmantonclassics.co.uk

XKs Unlimited (USA)
Tel: (001) 805 544 7864
Website: www.xks.com

LANCIA

Betacar
Tel: 01535 275560
Website: www.betacar.co.uk

Fulvia Sport
Tel: 01380 812283
Website: www.lanciafulviasport.com

Omicron
Tel: 01508 570351
Website: www.omicron.uk.com

LOTUS

Castle Lotus
Tel: 01279 647776
Website: www.castlelotus.com

Morland Jones
Tel: 0208 741 2303
Website: www.lotusservice.com

Paul Matty Sports Cars
Tel: 01527 835656
Website: www.paulmattysportscars.co.uk

PNM Engineering
Tel: 0151 630 6101
Website: www.pnmengineering.com

SJ Sportscars
Tel: 01363 777790
Website: www.sjsportscars.co.uk

Speedwell Automotive
Tel: 01425 477788
Website: www.speedwellautomotive.com

UK Sports Cars
Tel: 01227 728190
Website: www.uksportscars.com

MAZDA MX-5

Bourne Road Garage
Tel: 01322 521595
Website: www.mx5-mazda.co.uk

David Manners
Tel: 0121 544 4444
Website: www.davidmanners.co.uk

Moss Europe
Tel: 0800 281182
Website: www.moss-europe.co.uk

MX5 Parts
Tel: 0845 345 2384
Website: www.mx5parts.co.uk

Paul Sheard Autos
Tel: 01260 279797
Website: www.paulsheardautos.com

Sam Goodwin
Tel: 02476 353909
Website: www.samgoodwin.com

MERCEDES-BENZ

Autobarn
Tel: 01892 771321
Website: www.auto-barn.co.uk

Charles Ironside
Tel: 01730 828146
Website: www.charlesironside.co.uk

Mercedes-Crawley
Tel: 01932 569967
Website: www.mercedes-crawley.com

Prestige Motor Company
Tel: 01295 250222
Website: www.prestigemotorcompany.co.uk

Silchester Garage (SL specialists)
Tel: 0118 970 1648
Website: www.silchestergarage.co.uk

Silver Arrows Automobiles
Tel: 0208 789 8525
Website: www.silverarrows.co.uk

MG

Andy King MGs (pre-1955 models)
Tel: 01949 860519
Website: www.mgsparesandrestoration.com

Barry Walker (pre-war models)
Tel: 01789 400181
Website: www.barrywalker.com

Beech Hill Garage
Tel: 08701 203045
Website: www.beechhillgarage.com

Bob West (MGA sales)
Tel: 01977 703828
Website: www.bobwestclassiccars.co.uk

Brown & Gammons
Tel: 01462 490049
Website: www.ukmgparts.com

Bucks Sports & Classic Car Centre
Tel: 01296 433550
Website: www.mgsonthenet.co.uk

CCHL
Tel: 01482 441551
Website: www.cchl.co.uk

Colne Classics
Tel: 01255 432693
Website: www.colneclassics.com

Croydon Classics
Tel: 0208 407 2236
Website: www.croydonclassics.com

Cunliffes Garage
Tel: 01253 391466
Website: www.cunliffesgarage.co.uk

David Manners
Tel: 0121 544 4444
Website: www.davidmanners.co.uk

Former Glory
Tel: 0208 991 1963
Website: www.former-glory.com

Halls Garage
Tel: 01778 570286
Website: www.hallsgarage.co.uk

Leacy MG
Tel: 0121 356 3003
Website: www.leacymg.co.uk

MG Mecca
Tel: 01953 717100
Website: www.mgmecca.co.uk

MG Motorsport
Tel: 01442 832019
Website: www.mgmotorsport.com

The MGB Hive
Tel: 01945 700500
Website: www.mgbhive.co.uk

Mike Authers Classic Midgets
Tel: 01235 834664
Website: www.mgmidgets.com

Mike Rolls
Tel: 01258 820337
Website: www.mikerolls4mgs.co.uk

Moss Europe
Tel: 0800 281182
Website: www.moss-europe.co.uk

Peter Edney
Tel: 01279 826102
Website: www.peteredney.co.uk

SMR
Tel: 01707 876089
Website: www.mgsforsale.com

Snowdens of Harrogate (MGB specialists)
Tel: 01423 502406
Website: www.snowdensmgs.com

Sports Car Supplies
Tel: 0191 496 0522
Website: www.sportscarsupplies.co.uk

Surrey Sports & Classics
Tel: 01483 223830
Website: www.mgspares.co.uk

The Welsh MG Centre
Tel: 01978 263445
Website: www.welshmg.co.uk

MORGAN

Allon White
Tel: 0870 112 0872
Website: www.allonwhite.co.uk

Berry Brook
Tel: 01392 833301
Website: www.berrybrook.co.uk

Brands Hatch Morgans
Tel: 01732 882017
Website: www.morgan-cars.com

FH Douglass
Tel: 0208 567 0570
Website: www.fhdouglass.co.uk

Harpers
Tel: 01923 260299
Website: www.harpers-morgan.com

Heart of England Morgans
Tel: 01299 250141
Website: www.heartofenglandmorgans.co.uk

Lifes Motors
Tel: 01704 531375
Website: www.lifesmotors.com

Melvyn Rutter
Tel: 01279 725725
Website: www.melvyn-rutter.co.uk

Mole Valley Motor Group
Tel: 0208 394 1114
Website: www.mole-valley.co.uk

Richard Thorne Classic Cars
Tel: 0118 983 1200
Website: www.rtcc.co.uk

SGT
Tel: 01628 605353
Website: www.sgt.co.uk

Simmonds of Malvern
Tel: 01684 310688
Website: www.simmonds.uk.com

Stratton Motor Company
Tel: 01508 530491
Website: www.strattonmotorcompany.com

Thomson & Potter
Tel: 01828 670247
Website: www.morgansinscotland.co.uk

Wykehams
Tel: 0207 589 6894
Website: www.wykehams.co.uk

PORSCHE

Autobahn
Tel: 08456 444993
Website: www.autobahn.co.uk

Autofarm
Tel: 01865 331234
Website: www.autofarm.co.uk

BS Motorsport
Tel: 01296 658422
Website: www.bsmotorsport.co.uk

Charles Ivey
Tel: 0207 731 3612
Website: www.charlesivey.com

Chris Turner Porsche
Tel: 0208 451 6000
Website: www.christurner.com

Export 56
Tel: 01908 216661
Website: www.export56.com

Fuchs Porschebroker
Tel: 01623 411111
Website: www.fuchs.co.uk

Gantspeed Engineering
Tel: 01507 568474
Website: www.gantspeed.co.uk

John Mitchells Garage
Tel: 01202 462951
Website: www.9xx.co.uk

Northway Independent Porsche Specialists
Tel: 01189 714333
Website: www.northwayporsche.co.uk

Paragon Porsche
Tel: 01825 830424
Website: www.paragon.gb.com

Parr Porsche
Tel: 01293 537911
Website: www.parr-uk.co.uk

Wrightune Engineering
Tel: 01491 826911
Website: www.wrightune.co.uk

RELIANT SCIMITAR

Graham Walker
Tel: 01244 381777
Website: www.grahamwalker.co.uk

Queensberry Road Garage
Tel: 01536 513351
Website: www.qrgservices.co.uk

SMART ROADSTER

cambridge smart cars
Tel: 01223 881517
Website: www.cambridgesmartcars.co.uk

parts4smarts (Germany)
Tel: (0049) 6131 6 90 02 20
Website: www.parts4smarts.de

smarts-R-us
Tel: 0115 956 7896
Website: www.smartsrus.com

smart store
Tel: 0870 600 1828
Website: www.smartstore.co.uk

smart tune
Tel: 0870 880 3430
Website: www.smarttune.co.uk

SW-Exclusive (Germany)
Tel: (0049) 6112 3 67 19 5
Website: www.sw-exclusive.de

SUNBEAM ALPINE/TIGER

Sunbeam Spares Company
Tel: 01207 581025
Website: www.subeamsparescompany.com

TRIUMPH

David Manners
Tel: 0121 544 4444
Website: www.davidmanners.co.uk

James Paddock Triumph Spares
Tel: 01244 399899
Website: www.jamespaddock.co.uk

Kingston Sports Cars
Tel: 01359 269777
Website: www.kingstonsportscars.com

Midland Triumph Sales
Tel: 01543 481971
Mobile: 07709 874262

Moss Europe
Tel: 0800 281182
Website: www.moss-europe.co.uk

Quiller Triumph
Tel: 0208 854 4777
Website: www.quillertriumph.co.uk

Racetorations
Tel: 01427 616565
Website: www.racetorations.co.uk

Rees Bros
Tel: 01252 323038
Website: www.reesbros.co.uk

Revington TR
Tel: 01823 698437
Website: www.revingtontr.com

Rimmer Bros
Tel: 01522 568000
Website: www.rimmerbros.co.uk

Robsport International
Tel: 01763 262263
Website: www.robsport.co.uk

Southern Triumph Services
Tel: 01202 423687
Website: www.southerntriumph.com

Sports Car Supplies
Tel: 0191 496 0522
Website: www.sportscarsupplies.co.uk

SS Preparations (TR7/TR8)
Tel: 01706 874874
Website: www.ss-preparations.co.uk

TR Bitz
Tel: 01925 861861
Website: www.trbitz.com

TR GB
Tel: 01487 842168
Email: trgbltd@btconnect.com

TR Improvements
Tel: 01371 870175
Email: trimprovements@btopenworld.com

TR Shop London
Tel: 0208 995 6621
Website: www.trshop.co.uk

Triumph Nuts
Tel: 01925 732815
Website: www.triumphnuts.co.uk

Wins International
Tel: 01342 836060
Website: www.winsandco.co.uk

TRIUMPH STAG

Cherished Classics
Tel: 0116 276 2121
Website: www.cherishedclassics.co.uk

E.J. Ward
Tel: 0116 279 9060
Website: www.ejward.co.uk

Spring Grange Classics
Tel: 0116 259 5464
Website: www.springgrangeclassics.co.uk

The Stag Workshop
Tel: 01202 731570

TVR

David Gerald TVR Sportscars
Tel: 01386 793237
Website: www.davidgeraldtvr.com

Fernhurst Motor Company
Tel: 01428 653924
Website: www.fernhurst-tvr.co.uk

Mole Valley Motor Group
Tel: 0208 394 1114
Website: www.mole-valley.co.uk

Offord Motor Company
Tel: 01480 811484
Website: www.offord-motor.co.uk

Racing Green TVR
Tel: 01252 544888
Website: www.racinggreentvr.com

RT Racing
Tel: 0114 281 7507
Website: www.rtracing.co.uk

TVRfix
Tel: 0208 394 2847
Website: www.tvrfix.co.uk

Webbs Autos Specialist Cars
Tel: 01275 856666
Website: www.tvrspecialist.co.uk

Clubs, insurance, and contacts

SPORTS CAR CLUBS

AC Owners' Club
8 Nether Way
Upper Poppleton
York YO2 6JQ (UK)
Website: www.racecar.co.uk/acoc

Alfa Romeo
Alfa Romeo Owners' Club
47 Water Street
Lavenham
Suffolk CO10 9RN (UK)
Tel: (0044) 1787 249285
Website: www.aroc-uk.com

American Auto Club UK
Cartrefle
Pant Glas
Garndolbenmaen
Gwynedd LL51 9DJ (UK)
Tel: 0845 644 0345
Website: www.aac-uk.com

Aston Martin Owners' Club Ltd
Drayton St Leonard
Wallingford
Oxfordshire OX10 7BG (UK)
Tel: (0044) 1353 777353
Website: www.amoc.org

Audi TT Car Club of America
Website: www.audittcca.com

The (Audi) TT Owners' Club
PO Box 8061
Reading
Berkshire RG30 9BU
Website: www.ttoc.co.uk

Austin-Healey Club
4 Saxby Street
Leicester LE2 0ND (UK)
Tel: (0044) 116 254 4111
Website: www.austin-healey-club.com

Berkeley Enthusiasts' Club
41 Gorsewood Road
St Johns
Woking
Surrey GU21 1UZ (UK)

BMW Car Club
PO Box 328
Melksham
Wiltshire SN12 8SQ (UK)
Tel: (0044) 1225 709009

Bugatti Owners' Club
Prescott Hill
Gotherington
Cheltenham
Gloucestershire GL51 4RD (UK)

Classic Corvette Club UK
Roselea
Catwick Lane
Long Riston
East Riding HU11 5JR (UK)
Tel: (0044) 1964 501325
Website: www.corvetteclub.org.uk

Classic Jaguar Association
3530 W Garry Santa Ana
California 92704 (USA)
Tel: (001) 949 8371133
Website: www.classicjaguar.org

(Daihatsu) Copen Owners' Club
Website: www.copenownersclub.org.uk

Daimler SP 250 Register
PO Box 246
Dorking
Surrey RH5 5FU (UK)
Tel: (0044) 7885 882416
Website: www.dloc.org.uk

Ferrari Owners' Club
35 Market Place
Snettisham
Kings Lynn
Norfolk PE31 7LR (UK)
Tel: (0044) 1485 544500
Website: www.ferrariownersclub.co.uk

(Fiat) Barchetta UK Owners' Club
39 New Road
Great Kingshill
High Wycombe
Buckinghamshire HP15 6DR (UK)
Tel: (0044) 1494 713959
Website: www.fiatbarchetta.com/club/uk

Fiat Motor Club (GB)
45 Connaught Gardens
Muswell Hill
London N10 3LG (UK)
Tel: (0044) 208 372 4028
Website: www.fiatmotorclubgb.com

Fiat X1/9 Owners' Club
Bwthyn Penygroes
Penisarwaun
Caernarfon
Gwynedd L55 3PP (UK)
Tel: (0044) 1286 872161
Website: www.x1-9ownersclub.org.uk

Golden Gate Lotus Club
PO Box 117303
Burlingame
California 94011 (USA)
Website: www.gglotus.org

Historic Lotus Register
1 Cuckoo Mills
Meadowside Road
Falmouth
Cornwall TR11 4HZ (UK)
Tel: (0044) 1326 317789
Website: www.historiclotusregister.co.uk

Historic Sports Car Club
Swindon Road
Kington Langley
Nr Chippenham
Wiltshire SN15 5LY (UK)
Tel: (0044) 1249 758175

Honda International Sports Car Club
1 Wales Street
Watersheddings
Oldham
Lancashire OL1 4ET (UK)

Honda S800 Sports Car Club
60 Chesterwood Road
Kings Heath
Birmingham B13 0QE (UK)
Tel: (0044) 121 444 2988
Website: www.honda-S800-club.freeserve.co.uk

Honda S2000 Owners' Club
PO Box 2000
Rickmansworth
Hertfordshire WD3 9WX (UK)
Tel: (0044) 70992 279824
Website: www.s2kuk.com

Irish Jaguar & Daimler Club Ltd
Gleninagh
18 Cedarmount Road
Mount Merrion
Dublin (Ireland)
Website: www.irishjagclub.ie

Jaguar Association Germany
Zur Schleie 5
Überlingen D-88662 (Germany)
Tel: (0049) 7551 849147
Website: www.jaguar-association.de

Jaguar Drivers' Club
Jaguar House
18 Stuart Street
Luton
Bedfordshire LU1 2SL (UK)
Tel: (0044) 1582 419332

Jaguar Enthusiasts' Club Ltd
The Old Library
113A Gloucester Road North
Filton
Bristol BS34 7PU (UK)
Tel: (0044) 8708 452482

Jaguar E-Type Club
PO Box 2
Tenbury Wells
Worcestershire WR15 8XX (UK)
Tel: (0044) 1584 781588
Website: www.e-typeclub.com

Jensen Owners' Club
2 Westgate
Fulshaw Park
Wilmslow
Cheshire SK9 1QQ (UK)
Tel: (0044) 1625 525699

Lancia Motor Club
PO Box 51
Wrexham
Clwyd LL11 5ZE (UK)
Tel: (0044) 1270 620072
Website: www.lanciamotorclub.co.uk

Lotus 7 Club (including Caterhams)
PO Box 137
Alton
Hampshire GU34 5YH (UK)
Tel: 07000 572582
Website: www.lotus7club.co.uk

Club Lotus
41 Norwich Street
Dereham
Norfolk NR19 1AD (UK)
Tel: (0044) 1362 694459
Website: www.clublotus.co.uk

Lotus Car Club of British Columbia
PO Box 125
3456 Dunbar Street
Vancouver
British Columbia V6S 2C2 (Canada)
Website: www.geocities.com/lotusclubofbc

Lotus Club Online
14 Queens Park
Chester-le-Street
Durham DH3 3PL (UK)
Tel: (0044) 7766 444339
Website: www.lotusclubonline.co.uk

Lotus Drivers' Club
45 Barton Road
Harlington
Bedfordshire LU5 6LG (UK)
Tel: (0044) 1727 838015
Website: www.lotusdriversclub.org

Maserati Club
2 Sunny Bank
Widmer End
Buckinghamshire HP15 6PA (UK)
Tel: (0044) 1494 717701
Website: www.maseraticlub.co.uk

Mazda Rotary Club
41 Elizabeth Court
St James Road
Gravesend
Kent DA11 0HH (UK)
Tel: (0044) 1474 333099
Website: www.mazdarotaryclub.com

Mercedes-Benz Club
Unit 1
Woodside Farm Industrial Estate
Empingham
Rutland LE15 8QD (UK)
Tel: (0044) 7071 818868
Website: www.mercedes-benzownersclub.co.uk

Mercedes-Benz Owners' Association
Mercedes House
Langton Road
Langton Green
Tunbridge Wells
Kent TN3 0EG (UK)
Tel: (0044) 1892 860925
Website: www.mercedesclub.org.uk

MG Car Club
Kimber House
PO Box 251
Abingdon
Oxfordshire OX14 1FF (UK)
Tel: (0044) 1235 555552
Website: www.mgcars.org.uk/carclub

MG Octagon Car Club (pre-1956 MGs)
Unit 1/2
Parchfields Enterprise Park
Parchfields Farm
Colton Road
Trent Valley
Rugeley
Staffordshire WS15 3HB (UK)
Tel: (0044) 1889 574666
Website: www.mgoctagoncarclub.com

MG Owners' Club
Octagon House
Station Road
Swavesey
Cambridgeshire CB4 5QZ (UK)
Tel: (0044) 1954 231125
Website: www.mgownersclub.co.uk

Midget & Sprite Club
7 Kings Avenue
Hanham
Bristol BS15 3JN (UK)
Website: www.mgcars.org.uk/midgetspriteclub

Club MGF
Cavendish House
Queen Street
Mirfield
West Yorkshire WF14 8AH (UK)
Website: www.club-mgf.com

Morgan Sports Car Club
7 Woodland Grove
Gornal Wood
Dudley
West Midlands DY3 2XB (UK)
Tel: (0044) 1384 254480

MX-5 Ireland Owners' Club
12 Silver Birches
Millfarm
Dunboyne
County Meath (Ireland)
Website: www.mx5ireland.com

MX-5 Owners' Club
Kernshill
Shute Street
Stogumber
Taunton
Somerset TA4 3TU (UK)
Tel: 0845 601 4231
Website: www.mx5oc.co.uk

Panther Car Club Ltd
2 Ferndale Avenue
Stockport
Cheshire SK2 7DW (UK)
Tel: (0044) 161 483 9304
Website: www.panthercarclub.com

Panther Enthusiasts' Club UK
91 Fleet Road
Cove
Farnborough
Hampshire GU14 9RE (UK)
Tel: (0044) 1252 540217
Website: www.pantherclub.co.uk

Porsche Club of Great Britain
Cornbury House
Cotswold Business Village
Moreton-in-the-Marsh
Gloucestershire GL56 0JQ (UK)
Tel: (0044) 1608 652911

Porsche Enthusiasts' Club (Independent)
31 The Grove
Hartlepool
Cleveland TS26 9LZ (UK)
Tel: 07000 924968
Website: www.tipec.org.uk

Reliant Sabre & Scimitar Owners' Club
PO Box 67
Teddington
Middlesex TW11 8QR (UK)
Tel: (0044) 208 977 6625
Website: www.scimitarweb.com

The Smart Club
Tel: (0044) 870 199 6423
www.thesmartclub.co.uk

Sunbeam Alpine Owners' Club
PO Box 226
Grimsby DN37 0GG (UK)
Website: www.saoc.demon.co.uk

Sunbeam Tiger Owners' Club
8 Villa Real Estate
Consett
Durham DH8 6BJ (UK)
Tel: (0044) 1207 508296
Website: www.sunbeamtiger.co.uk

Suzuki Cappuccino Owners' Club
2 Marlborough Rise
Camberley
Surrey GU15 2ED (UK)
Tel: (0044) 1276 503630
Website: www.score.org.uk

Toyota MR2 Mk I Club
41 Waysbrook
Letchworth
Hertfordshire SG6 2DT (UK)
Tel: (0044) 1462 671897
Website: www.mr2mk1club.com

(Toyota) MR2 Drivers' Club
PO Box 999
Huntingdon
Cambridgeshire PE28 2PX (UK)
Tel: (0044) 1487 710010
Website: www.mr2dc.com

(Toyota) MR2 Owners' Club
Website: www.mr2oc.co.uk

(Toyota) MR2 Roadster Owners' Club
Website: www.mr2roc.org

TR Register
1B Hawksworth
Southmead Industrial Park
Didcot
Oxfordshire OX11 7HR (UK)
Tel: (0044) 1235 818866
Website: www.tr-register.co.uk

Club Triumph
Freepost (SWB 20389)
Christchurch
Dorset BH23 6ZZ (UK)
Tel: (0044) 1425 274193
Website: www.club.triumph.org.uk

Triumph Roadster Club
Oak Tree Farm
Anstye
Haywards Heath
West Sussex RH17 5AH (UK)
Website: www.triumphroadster.org

Triumph Sporting Owners' Club
57 Rothiemey Road
Flixton
Urmston
Manchester M31 3JY (UK)
Tel: (0044) 161 747 3618

Triumph Sports Six Club
Main Street
Lubenham
Leicestershire LE16 9TF (UK)
Tel: (0044) 1858 434424
Website: www.tssc.org.uk

(Triumph) Stag Owners' Club
The Old Rectory
Aslacton
Norfolk NR15 2JN (UK)
Tel: (0044) 7071 224245
Website: www.stag.org.uk

Triumph Stag Enthusiasts
44 Deans Way
Edgware
Middlesex HA8 9NJ (UK)
Tel: (0044) 208 959 4731
Website: www.brmmbrmm.com/trstagenth

Triumph Stag Register
12 Holly Lodge
Lindsay Road
Poole
Dorset BH13 6BQ (UK)
Tel: (0044) 1202 761051
Website: www.tristagreg.org

TVR Car Club
Unit 5
Nova House
Audley Avenue Enterprise Park
Newport
Shropshire TF10 7DW (UK)
Tel: (0044) 1952 822126
Website: www.tvrcc.com

Vauxhall VX220 & Opel Speedster Group
c/o Club Lotus
41 Norwich Street
Dereham
Norfolk NR19 1AD
Tel: (0044) 1362 691144

Vintage Sports Car Club
The Old Post Office
West Street
Chipping Norton
Oxfordshire OX7 5EL (UK)
Tel: (0044) 1608 644777
Website: www.vscc.co.uk

MAGAZINES

Most magazines featuring sports cars also tend to offer coverage of other vehicles – for example, the entire classic scene rather than simply classic sports cars. However, the following titles all have regular sports car editorial. This is by no means a full list of magazines featuring sports cars, but it will give you an idea of the principal magazines (and their websites) available at the time of writing.

UK
Auto Express
(www.autoexpress.co.uk)

Autocar
(www.autocarmagazine.co.uk)

Car
(www.carmagazine.co.uk)

Classic Car Mart
(www.classic-car-mart.co.uk)

Classic Car Weekly
(www.classic-car-weekly.co.uk)

Classic Cars
(www.classiccarsmagazine.co.uk)

Classic & Sports Car
(www.classicandsportscar.com)

Octane
(www.octane-magazine.com)

Practical Classics
(www.practicalclassics.co.uk)

Top Gear
(www.topgear.com)

What Car?
(www.whatcar.com)

USA and Canada
AutoWeek (USA)
(www.autoweek.com)

Canadian Classics & Performance (Canada)
(www.canadianclassicsmag.com)

Car & Driver (USA)
(www.caranddriver.com)

Car Collector Magazine (USA)
(www.carcollector.com)

Classic Motorsports Magazine (USA)
(www.classicmotorsports.net)

Motor Trend (USA)
(www.motortrend.com)

Sports Car Market (USA)
(www.sportscarmarket.com)

Europe
Auto Bild (Germany)
(www.autobild.de)

Auto Motor Und Sport (Germany)
(www.auto-motor-und-sport.de)

Auto News (Germany)
(www.auto-news.de)

Auto Zeitung (Germany)
(www.autozeitung.de)

L'Automobile (France)
(www.automobilemagazine.com)

SPORTS CAR INSURANCE

Looking for competitively priced insurance for your sports car in the UK? While mainstream insurance companies usually offer good deals, owners of older, modified, or unusual sports cars often prefer to deal with more specialist insurance companies. The following insurers and brokers can arrange specialist cover for both classic and modern sports cars, incorporating such features as agreed-value policies for older models or limited-mileage policies for cars that aren't used on an everyday basis. Contact them direct for an individual quotation.

Adrian Flux
Tel: 0845 130 3400
Website: www.adrianflux.co.uk

AON
Tel: 08705 70 80 90
Website: www.aon.co.uk

Carole Nash
Tel: 0800 781 9289
Website: www.carolenash.com

Firebond
Tel: 0870 111 0465
Website: www.firebond.co.uk

Footman James
Tel: 0845 458 6776
Website: www.footmanjames.co.uk

Heritage Insurance
Tel: 0845 811 8118
Website: www.heritage-quote.co.uk

Lancaster Insurance
Tel: 01480 484848
Website: www.lancasterinsurance.co.uk

MCE
Tel: 0870 90 90 911
Website: www.insurancemce.com

Performance Direct
Tel: 0870 458 4074
Website: www.performancedirect.co.uk

Peter Best Insurance Services
Tel: 0845 130 0045
Website: www.peterbestinsurance.co.uk

RH Specialist Car Insurance
Tel: 01277 206911
Website: www.rhclassicinsurance.co.uk

Roadsure
Tel: 0845 408 0016
Website: www.roadsure.com

Sureterm Direct
Tel: 0845 20 20 230
Website: www.sureterm.co.uk

Towergate Hall & Clarke
Tel: 0870 990 6060

Index